# discover
# counselling

Aileen Milne

For UK order enquiries: please contact Bookpoint Ltd,
130 Milton Park, Abingdon, Oxon OX14 4SB.
*Telephone*: +44 (0) 1235 827720. *Fax*: +44 (0) 1235 400454.
Lines are open 09.00–17.00, Monday to Saturday, with a 24-hour
message answering service. Details about our titles and how to
order are available at www.hoddereducation.com

*British Library Cataloguing in Publication Data*: a catalogue record
for this title is available from the British Library.

First published in UK 2011 by Hodder Education, part of Hachette UK,
338 Euston Road, London NW1 3BH.

Typeset by MPS Limited, a Macmillan Company.

Printed in Great Britain for Hodder Education, an Hachette UK Company,
338 Euston Road, London NW1 3BH, by CPI Cox & Wyman, Reading,
Berkshire RG1 8EX.

The publisher has used its best endeavours to ensure that the URLs
for external websites referred to in this book are correct and active
at the time of going to press. However, the publisher and the author
have no responsibility for the websites and can make no guarantee
that a site will remain live or that the content will remain relevant,
decent or appropriate.

Hachette UK's policy is to use papers that are natural, renewable
and recyclable products and made from wood grown in sustainable
forests. The logging and manufacturing processes are expected to
conform to the environmental regulations of the country of origin.

Impression number   10 9 8 7 6 5 4 3 2 1
Year                2015 2014 2013 2012 2011

# Contents

Mr J.L Shash
Library

# 1

# *the counselling role*

Counselling is a widespread practice in contemporary society. Emotional turmoil and unhappiness are no longer usually viewed as a 'moral' or 'psychological' failing but as a possible – if not probable – part of everyone's life experience as they grow, age and develop. Counselling can be a way of helping a person through these difficult challenges and crises as well as a means to develop their self-awareness and to deepen their capacity to enjoy life and to conduct fulfilling human relationships.

This chapter looks in outline at how the professional counsellor differs from the psychotherapist on the one hand and the friend in whom one confides on the other, as well as at the similarities that these roles can share. As we shall see throughout this book, empathy, confidentiality, trust and a clear understanding of working parameters are key to the successful practice of counselling at every level.

Counselling can take many forms: people receive counselling individually, or have couple counselling or family counselling — when the dynamics between family members will be the focus of the work. The capacity and setting in which counsellors work also varies, ranging from a few hours a week doing voluntary work with an agency or organization to working privately in a professional practice. Some counselling involves working with particular client groups — examples are student counselling and marriage counselling; and some focus on particular problems — for example, medical conditions such as cancer or AIDS, or social problems such as alcohol or drug abuse. To add to the complexity, there are many 'schools' of counselling, which are informed by their own particular theoretical frameworks. These can, however, be identified and understood by the three core approaches of analytical, humanistic and behavioural perspectives and these will be explored in later chapters.

Many of us no longer live in supportive communities bound together by religious faith and beliefs. Our world horizons have expanded; the cities where many of us live can feel large and impersonal. Perhaps in seeking counselling we attempt to repersonalize our lives. We take our problems to a place where we feel we will be listened to and where our thoughts and feelings are regarded as important. The role of counselling is ever evolving to meet the challenges of modern social pressures and demands, which we often attempt to deal with at cost to our inner world.

We enter into a counselling relationship when we engage the help of a counsellor in mutual agreement. No one can be forced into a counselling–client relationship; a person chooses to have counselling, otherwise it isn't counselling at all. The activity of counselling has been defined in many ways. The following are some of the ways that counselling can help people resolve problems or help people live their lives in a more insightful, fulfilling way. Counselling can help people:

* to clarify what's important in their lives
* to get in touch with their inner resources

* in the exploration of feelings, thoughts and meanings particular to them
* by offering support at times of crisis
* by offering support during developmental and transitional periods
* to work through 'stuck' issues – this might involve integrating childhood experiences
* to reach a resolution of problems.

## *Psychotherapy and counselling: where they converge and where they differ*

The terms 'counselling', 'psychotherapy' and 'therapy' often seem to be used in an interchangeable way, their differences unclear to the uninitiated. In particular, the use of the term 'therapy' is widespread. A dictionary of psychology would define therapy using the words: 'treatment of disease or disorder' and 'to make better'. If we look at the word 'disease' in two parts, *dis* and *ease*, we see that it refers to the state of a person who is no longer at ease with themselves in their physical and/or psychological state. Therapy, or counselling, is a process that helps the client make their life better by focusing on the areas of their lives that cause them problems or distress.

The word 'therapy' has come to be a generic term used to describe something that is helpful or nurturing in some way or that gives relief from the strains of everyday life, hence such terms as 'retail therapy'. It's also used as an abbreviated form of 'psychotherapy'. The word 'therapist' is used likewise as an abbreviated form of 'psychotherapist', but many counsellors also refer to themselves as therapists.

### Similarities between psychotherapy and counselling

Psychotherapy and counselling are regarded as separate professions. They sometimes have their own, and sometimes share, professional associations that safeguard the interests of both clients and practitioners. Among the functions that these professional associations serve is the accreditation of training courses and the accreditation of individual practitioners.

Although they have separate identities in the field of therapy, it's a widely held view that there's a lot of overlap between the two. Both use a similar theoretical framework of reference; the same training materials, books and resources are used on courses. This is particularly true when courses are based around the same theoretical 'school' or approach; for example, person-centred or psychodynamic. A person may reach professional status as either a person-centred counsellor or psychotherapist, yet their fundamental differences are unclear. Members of both professions work in similar settings, in medical and health centres, doctors' surgeries and clinics, and this can add to the confusion.

## Differences between psychotherapy and counselling

### Length and depth of training

Whereas to reach a professional level a counsellor would most likely be expected to train for a period of two to three years part-time, a psychotherapist would have spent a minimum of three years and often longer in training. Psychotherapy training often incorporates a year of working in a health care setting or private practice towards the end of the course, providing case study material for assessment.

### Origins

Psychotherapy has been a branch of medicine from the late nineteenth century and psychoanalysis was a major development in psychotherapy in the twentieth century. In the early 1900s another type of psychotherapy (called behaviourism) associated therapy with psychology and science, mainly because its theories were developed from behavioural experiments. In contrast, counselling is a comparatively new discipline that was developed by psychotherapists such as Carl Rogers in America in the late 1950s.

Counselling began in educational settings and was widely applied in marriage guidance, pastoral care and voluntary organizations. It subsequently developed into private practice.

**Length of treatment**

It's generally thought that psychotherapists work long term with clients while counsellors work short term, or in crisis situations. There are no hard and fast rules. Counselling can incorporate both short-term and long-term ways of working; it sometimes begins with a short-term focus and for various reasons results in long-term therapy. Long-term counselling is common and, conversely, it's not uncommon for psychotherapists to offer brief psychotherapy.

**Depth of work**

The extended training of the psychotherapist is designed to equip them to work in more depth with clients. However, although this is used as a focus of training, it's not always the case that psychotherapists exclusively cater for the client with more difficulties. It does seem true to say, as a general rule, that while the counsellor sees a client once a week for a single session, the psychotherapist might see a client two or more times in a week.

**Personal therapy for trainees**

Both professions require trainees to have personal therapy for the duration of the course. A psychotherapist in training, who is expecting to see individual clients two or more times a week, is usually required by the conditions of their course to have the corresponding amount of personal therapy throughout the training. The same applies to the counsellor who's training with a view to seeing individuals once a week; they too will require personal therapy once a week for the duration of the course, although this requirement doesn't necessarily apply to shorter courses.

## *The counselling role*

Counselling can take many forms:
* Doctors refer patients to counsellors who practise alongside them in their surgeries.

* Teachers and youth workers will often direct young people to counselling agencies for help.
* Counsellors are called to accidents and disaster areas to counsel the victims and their families.
* Individuals seek counselling for themselves for all kinds of reasons.
* Counselling is used in a variety of settings: in education, in pastoral care and increasingly in industry.

The role counselling plays in society is increasingly multifaceted and always supportive. Counselling now seems to be very much a part of our lives, no longer regarded as a luxury or indulgence.

**Roles within roles**

So that we can make informed choices about how we would like to get involved in counselling, it's important to make distinctions between the different roles of counselling.

There are three different ways:

1 As a professional, which will usually require two to three years of study to acquire knowledge of skills, theory and practical experience.
2 By working in the voluntary sector within an organization that will offer training, sometimes in a specialist area.
3 As part of a job, probably using basic skills to enhance communication and listening/responding abilities.

Other uses for acquired counselling skills are in personal development and learning how to be an effective supporter of colleagues, family and friends.

## Those who have counselling

Who has counselling?
* From a counsellor's perspective, are those who have counselling different from you or me?
* Are they a certain type of person who is unable to cope as the rest of us do?

The answer to both these questions is usually 'No'. Often the problems clients bring to session are not outside our own life experiences. When they are, the counsellor would be wise to find out as much as possible about the subject or guide the client to an agency or a counsellor with expertise in the particular problem — for example, sexual abuse, a serious case of self-harming or a drug habit.

### Problems people take to counselling

People go to counselling for all kinds of reasons: following a bereavement or divorce, stress at work or school, depression or low self-esteem. There are many other factors that can leave people feeling alone and overwhelmed with hopelessness. When an individual seeks counselling it's because they have internal conflicts and pent-up feelings of some form that are spoiling their enjoyment of life.

## *The active listener*

Counsellors are commonly thought of as sympathetic professional 'listening ears' but, as I hope will become apparent, there are many skills involved. A trained and experienced counsellor is adept at *active* listening. They're actively involved in giving the client full attention and appropriate responses. This is a lot more complex than it first sounds.

## *The counsellor—client relationship*

Increasingly it's the relationship between the counsellor and client that's seen as crucial to a successful therapeutic process, more so than the counsellor's choice of theoretical background. Therapists such as Petruska Clarkson and Michael Khan see this working relationship as a fundamental determining factor in how much a client is able to benefit from therapy.

Generally speaking, whatever theories the counsellor is familiar with, the basic requisites are the same. These are that the counsellor provides an environment of privacy, safety and assured confidentiality, is non-defensive and shows respect for the client at all times.

A non-judgemental stance encourages an openness and an understanding to develop. Acceptance and empathy from the counsellor helps the client access their innermost feelings and inner resources. By their warm, accepting attitude towards clients, counsellors are conveying: 'I accept you; given what has happened to you in your life, it's understandable that you should feel the way you do or that you have behaved the way you have.' This is not token blanket approval of everything a client has felt or done, but is an empathic response, as if having walked in their shoes and felt what they have felt.

## Non-directive counselling

Most counsellors won't offer advice or tell the client what they should do, or take advantage in any way of the client, who is, after all, in a vulnerable position. Some forms of counselling are more directive or goal oriented than others but nevertheless the counsellor would never tell the client what to do; rather they would help clients to identify and clarify areas in their lives that they want to change and also help clients to tap into their own resources to find solutions.

## The working alliance

The working alliance is the agreement and established framework of the work that's mutually undertaken. A framework needs to be established at the onset in which both client and counsellor are in agreement about the ways they'll work together. This helps establish trust. The initial meeting is very important; both the client and counsellor are assessing whether or not they think they could work together.

## The 50-minute therapy hour

Usually a counsellor will agree to see a client for 50 minutes once a week at their work premises. The 50-minute session has become a tradition, to allow 50 minutes of undivided attention for the client followed by ten minutes' break for the counsellor, during which they can make a few notes about the session or to have a few minutes to relax between seeing clients. Some counsellors, however, prefer one-hour sessions.

## Confidentiality

A confidential setting provides the client with safety and privacy. In usual circumstances, confidentiality is upheld. To ensure anonymity clients' names are represented by a number or their initials only. Brief case notes might be written during or after a session but these will be destroyed in time. However, if a client tells the counsellor something that puts them or others in danger or is illegal, it would be irresponsible for the counsellor to hold on to this. Counsellors need to be aware of legal obligations and agency policies regarding, for example, disclosure of physical or sexual child abuse, when legal requirements demand that confidential information is made available. The client needs to be informed of any conditions and limitations of confidentiality at the onset of counselling.

# *The difference between a counsellor's role and that of a friend*

A friend, by the very nature of the relationship, has a vested interest. Something told to a friend could be embarrassing, shocking or hurtful to them. It might be something they feel ill-equipped to deal with, or involve mixed loyalties. Also, with friends we sometimes assume a persona that we feel is acceptable to them; for example, a mask that says, 'I'm a person who can cope with anything life throws at me,' or 'I'm always a helpful and kind person.' How can we then confide in a friend that we're not coping at all, or tell them that we're feeling annoyed with some people at the moment, including them?

A friend could agree not to tell anyone else something that's said in confidence but later, in a moment of weakness, or because they think it might be best to tell, for whatever reason, might go ahead and divulge a secret. The feelings of betrayal can be damaging to both individuals and their friendship.

To be in a position to help, a friend or family member needs to be aware of these and other possible pitfalls. The danger is that, as an unskilled helper, we leap in at times, realizing too late that we're ill-equipped and unable to cope with such a responsible position. The fact that we're emotionally involved with the person need not, however, be a drawback.

## A case study

Let's look at a hypothetical case study to see the possible benefits of counselling.

A middle-aged man, whom I'll call Colin, has come to counselling because he feels that he's not coping at the moment. He hasn't told anyone that he's sought help for himself in the form of counselling because it's a source of shame for him to admit that he doesn't feel in control of his life and he needs help. Colin was made redundant six months ago and, although he's been trying to establish himself as a freelance worker, prospective clients are prejudiced towards his age. At 52 years old Colin is feeling a failure – a 'has-been' with no useful future. His son too has his own problems with his marriage. Colin has never been one to confide in others, friends or family. He's always been the stoic provider, the reliable father and husband, and he's now feeling without a role in life. As a person who has rarely shown his emotions, he is now feeling 'all at sea'. In this frame of mind there really isn't anyone Colin feels he can share his feelings of inadequacy with. The image he thought others had of him was virtually all he had left to bolster his sinking self-esteem.

Colin felt that he'd nothing to lose by going to counselling. He had no image to live up to there. He could explore his feelings of inadequacy, shame and depression and growing sense of hopelessness.

With the help of his counsellor he was able to talk about his fears: of ageing, of feeling that he was of no use to anyone, of perhaps in the future being unable to look after himself or his family. Many issues came to the fore for Colin as he thought about his childhood and his overbearing father's expectations of him. He began to be aware of patterns in his life. He understood why he had always felt compelled to be an achiever and why he couldn't express or even access his emotions readily.

## Acquiring skills for personal use

An understanding of basic counselling skills can be useful to any relationship. This doesn't mean that by acquiring a few skills you'll be able to solve all the problems you have with those you care about or be equipped to work at the same depth as an experienced counsellor, but, by learning simple listening and responding techniques, you can improve how you communicate with others. The probable outcome of this is that relationships will improve.

The success of this kind of activity, to a certain extent, depends on our ability to put our own needs aside, but this can be viewed as a temporary situation. When we're able to listen to the distress of another human being and not heavily identify with, resist or take offence in relation to that distress in some way, we open channels of greater communication and in time it benefits everybody.

# 2

# *the counsellor's role*

In this chapter we look at the essential qualities that underpin effective, professional counselling – the necessary foundations for the skills that are acquired and developed during training and practice. A capacity for warmth, empathy and tolerance are key, as is a certain amount of 'life experience' – for this reason counsellors are unlikely to be very young and training courses may set a minimum age for candidates. Those assessing prospective counsellors' suitability for training will be looking for evidence of key qualities during the selection process.

Perhaps the most essential quality of any counsellor, however, is self-understanding – an objective grasp of one's own strengths and weaknesses, prejudices and biases, and the ways in which one's own life history may colour attitudes towards others. Self-understanding is a prerequisite to understanding – and helping – others. Therefore mostly counselling training recommends the experience of personal therapy and this can prove to be both challenging and rewarding.

Perhaps you're interested in getting involved with counselling in some capacity but aren't sure what it involves. You might doubt that you have the right qualities, or perhaps you're unsure how much you would be able to commit in terms of training and counselling hours, realizing how demanding this kind of work can be.

## Qualities of a counsellor

Counsellors are not super-beings who have a monopoly on emotional strength and wisdom. Although people often have the expectation that counsellors will 'sort out' their problems, it's the clients themselves, guided and encouraged by the counsellor, who do the work.

While a practising counsellor will retain theoretical knowledge as a backdrop, the most important factor is likely to be the time and attention they give to a client. Psychologist Carl Jung advised the therapist: 'Learn your theories as well as you can, but put them aside when you touch the miracle of the living soul.' This reminds us of the uniqueness of each one of us and suggests to us that no encounter with one person will be quite the same as with another. Clients, as individuals with individual problems, are the counsellor's primary concern.

While brainstorming in a training session, the trainer asked the participants what qualities we might expect in a counsellor and the following words and phrases were suggested. Some of the suggestions demonstrate the high expectations that the prospective counsellors had of themselves. They included:

*integrity, an ability to look at oneself, knowledge of theory, humility, empathy, a liking of others, an interest in people, kindness, non-judgemental attitude, respect for others, a good memory for detail, being a good listener, patience, sensitivity, in control of own emotions, professionalism, ethical behaviour.*

To have all of these attributes is a tall order. These are ideals that we probably feel we fall short of. As an afterthought, someone added: 'being courageous'. That seemed to resonate with the trainer, who smiled in agreement and commented that a counsellor does need courage to face the problems a client brings and to be in the experience with them.

Not everyone will be considered to be suitable counsellor material by those who select for organizations or training courses. The qualities they will be looking for include:

1 an ability to mix with others in an assessment situation (self-esteem and boundary issues)
2 an adaptability/spontaneity – able to respond to various set 'tasks'
3 an ability to self-assess
4 observational qualities – insightfulness
5 an ability to be themselves
6 evidence of warmth of character, e.g. empathic responding
7 the nominee being in a position in their life that isn't at odds with the demands of training.

Individuals assess their own suitability – some drop out of counselling at selection stage, deciding that it's not for them. Others leave at various stages of training. Still others choose to train in gradual stages in correlation with their own personal development.

## Creating core conditions

Of all the positive qualities already mentioned, the most important are generally considered to be encapsulated in the core conditions or values that originated from Carl Rogers' ideas of client-centred therapy, now more commonly referred to as person-centred therapy. These are congruence, unconditional positive regard and empathy; they can be abbreviated to CUE – a form that is easily remembered. Other terms that are sometimes used in connection with the core conditions are: non-possessive warmth, acceptance and a non-judgemental attitude. Genuineness is sometimes used instead of 'congruence'.

### Being non-judgemental

What does it mean to be non-judgemental towards another? Is it even possible, considering that we make decisions all the time about what we like, dislike, tolerate or enjoy about other people? To judge a person can mean to have an opinion about whether they're a good or bad person or whether we approve or disapprove of their behaviour. The stance we take towards others is often strongly related to our own conditioning and life experiences.

How then can a counsellor be any different? This can be more easily understood if we view the non-judgemental approach as a position taken outside ordinary social interaction. Rather than rigidly classifying someone's behaviour or opinions as 'good' or 'bad', we need to consider the whole person. We can then understand the privilege of our position and adopt a receptive, supportive attitude.

It's debatable whether we can ever truly sustain a non-judgemental approach with our clients. I personally see it as an ideal.

## Acceptance and self-development

It's considered important for counsellors to have personal therapy or counselling so that they can explore their own prejudices and unresolved emotional issues, which might otherwise get in the way of constructive work with a client. The much quoted words over the temple of Delphi, 'Know Thyself', have significance for any therapist. If we're aware of our own strengths and weaknesses, then we're more likely to understand the complexities and flaws of clients.

Personal therapy gradually helps us to become more comfortable around distress and strong emotions. How can we expect ourselves to be capable of 'holding' a client through their angry feelings if we haven't to some extent come to terms with our own anger?

## Life experience

The most useful experience of all for preparation as a counsellor is to have lived and learned. Our own life experience obviously gives us insight into the situations of others, although there's a dichotomy in this. It would be a mistake to assume that because we have had a similar experience – for example, a divorce or the death of a loved one – our responses would be exactly the same as another person's. When we give people our subjective views, we sometimes assume an authority and then we're unable to explore different options.

Counselling is one of the few vocations where getting older is not a problem. To come to counselling in our thirties, forties or at a greater age means we come with an abundance of life experience. Hopefully we have learned from experiences, good and bad. We've gone through difficult times that stretched our emotional and psychological resources and survived the trauma. Tutors and trainers in counselling look for evidence of resilience in prospective trainees.

## What do you want to get out of counselling?

People who become counsellors come from diverse backgrounds, such as business, teaching, nursing and social work. Some have initially taken up counselling on a voluntary basis or as an enhancement to their work. They become inspired by what they've learned, change track altogether and decide to train further to become professional counsellors or psychotherapists. Many people who become interested in counselling have had intensive therapy themselves. They've had first-hand experience as a client. They feel that therapy has been a positive experience and are consequently interested in pursuing counselling as a career. Others choose to work in areas where they themselves have suffered trauma.

## Commitments

Training as a professional counsellor can be a lengthy business. The more thoroughly we train the more commitment is involved in terms of time, finance and energy. Many people receive initial training through a counselling agency. Agencies usually offer training over a relatively short period of 10–12 weeks and after this the trainees begin to counsel clients in a voluntary capacity. Before embarking on the training, it could be useful to ask yourself a few questions:

* Why do I want to counsel other people?
* What do I want to get out of counselling?
* How much time can I give on a voluntary basis?
* Am I hoping to make a career out of counselling?
* Have I the financial resources to embark on a lengthy programme of learning?
* Am I willing to be personally challenged?

## *The emotional demands and rewards of personal growth*

Training as a counsellor requires a willingness to self-examine and to be open about ourselves. Even on the shortest courses, the trainee will be focusing on personal attitudes, values and feelings in relation to other people and their own lives. How can we have understanding of and empathy for other people if we have little understanding or tolerance of ourselves? In person-centred therapy the counsellor takes a stance of 'unconditional positive regard' towards the client. This is to be non-judgemental, accepting, warm and supportive. If we judge another person negatively we take a superior position to elevate ourselves. To take the role of empathic listener and supporter of another person requires us to drop these attitudes and recognize that we're all in the same position; we're all human. This requires a willingness to self-scrutinize and self-assess.

It's not difficult to see why self-exploration is challenging and demanding. It can also at times be frustrating, but sticking with it – what therapists call 'going with the process' – does yield rewards. Self-exploration through participating in therapy offers unique opportunities.

# 3

# *skills used in counselling*

This chapter considers the basic skills of counselling that you would expect to learn in theory and experience in practice if you attended any beginners' counselling training course. Understanding the way we can interact with people in a positive way in theory and becoming good at that interaction in practice are essential. A trainee counsellor will need to think carefully about the way that they ask questions – not as a way of prising out 'information' but as helpful signposts – and to become attuned to body language, their clients' as well as their own.

The role of a counsellor is much less intrusive than those new to the practice sometimes think. Ideally a counsellor gives their client the space and time to feel and reflect and provides the psychological 'head room' that enables the client to make their own discoveries and gain their own insights. A golden rule of counselling is to use your ears and eyes more than your mouth!

## Sharpening our awareness

Speaking, hearing, seeing, feeling and thinking are all ways we respond and give attention to each other. At times of emergency we often have a heightened response to other people in need; both head and heart go into operative mode. In our concern for the person, we examine the most effective way to help them find relief from their predicament and we're highly focused. At other times, especially when strong emotions are involved, we're often at a loss about how to be of any help to the distressed person. By identifying and developing simple skills, we can enhance our ability to be more fully present for another person when they're distressed or experiencing difficulties in their lives. Although some readers might be interested in acquiring skills as would-be helpers rather than counsellors, for the sake of clarity I use the terms 'counsellor' and 'client' to denote the different roles. It would be equally appropriate to use the terms 'helper' and colleague, friend or family member.

The basic skills that counsellors use involve listening, observing, attending and responding. Active listening requires full attention and alertness to every nuance, to what's both implicitly and openly said, thereby helping the client to understand their feelings and thoughts. The ground skills that enable us to respond effectively include reflecting (paraphrasing and summarizing), appropriate questioning and empathy. Responding on an empathic level involves responding to content – to what is being said – and to feelings, by tentatively reflecting back your understanding of what the client is expressing.

## Use of questions

Think about how you respond when others come to you for help, advice or general succour. Do you fire a lot of questions at them, questions such as: 'What's wrong?', 'Why are you so upset?', 'Is it something she or he has said to you?' Asking questions might seem the most natural thing to do on these occasions, but questioning can be off-putting if overdone. Questions can be intrusive and too forceful, and could be used to satisfy our own curiosity, rather than help the other person. Yet questions, used tentatively and sensitively, are necessary for the exploration and clarification of facts and feelings.

In counselling, questions tend to be used sparingly because clients are generally encouraged to tackle problems at their own pace. During therapy painful material inevitably surfaces and insensitive questioning from the therapist is likely to be destructive to building trust. One of the tenets of therapy is the belief that people can self-heal, that they possess an innate ability to recognize what they need and, given the right set of circumstances, they can reorientate themselves to what is meaningful in their lives. In other words, most of us don't want other people telling us what to do, nor do we want others delving nosily into our business, but we do appreciate someone being with us in our troubles and listening attentively with sensitivity while we make sense of our situation.

## Closed questions

When we ask a closed question, it is usually met with a closed response – a response that doesn't allow any further exploration. Closed questions are useful for information gathering when we need to know specific facts or specific information; for example, in an intake session with a new client when a counsellor notes things like marriage status, medical details, work details and so on; or in the case of a younger person details of school, college and whom they live with.

The answer to a closed question is often 'yes', 'no' or 'don't know'. The closed question begins: 'Do you', 'Can you', 'Have you', 'Is it', 'Would you say', 'Could it', 'Don't you think' and so on.

The problem with questioning that invites a 'yes' or 'no' type of reply is that it can leave both parties facing a blank wall and can lead only to more questioning. While you are bombarding someone with questions, their feelings are subdued.

## Open questions

Open questions are valuable because they enable the expression of thoughts, feelings and personal meanings. They invite the other person to talk, communicate and self-explore. They allow time to explore situations. Open questions begin with 'How', 'Where', 'When', 'What', 'In what way' and so forth. The answers given to questions like these allow the counsellor to have a clearer understanding and help the client to be more specific. Open questions have no 'right' answer.

## Multiple and frequent questions

Don't ask too many questions – be sparing. It's important to respect the client's right to privacy. Some issues could be delicate and too intimate to rush into. Allow time for trust to develop. The client might feel interrogated rather than supported, especially in the first few sessions when it's crucial to establish trust. It could impede the building of a rapport between you. The frequent use of questions doesn't allow time for the exploration of thoughts and feelings as and when they arise; therapy can then be experienced as confusing, as the counsellor's interest appears to be on a superficial level only.

## Leading questions

Leading questions imply answers that the questioner would find acceptable. Leading – or biased – questions can effectively stop clients expressing their thoughts and feelings for fear of ridicule. For example:

*'You're not thinking of leaving your children, are you?'*

*'You're not going to cry, are you?'*

These questions consist of an instructive statement: 'You wouldn't give up your job', followed by a question, 'Would you?' The first part indirectly tells the other person what to do, the second part appears to give an option. Empathic sensitive questioning is neither judgemental nor restrictive.

### Questions to ask about your questions

* Are you trying to clear up a point? (clarifying)
* Are you information gathering?
* Does the question help your client to explore self and situation?
* Does the question have any therapeutic value – i.e. helping in some way?
* Are you avoiding anything by asking a question? You might be filling a space, trying to put a client (who you might think is uncomfortable with silences) at ease, or perhaps you find it difficult to manage silences.

Asking too many questions can be an attempt to force change or to control the direction of the sessions; both can cause the client to deflect from issues rather than focus on them.

## *Use of empathy*

Empathy has been described in a number of ways: as if walking in another's shoes, entering into another person's frame of reference, or having the ability to experience life as the other person does by temporarily entering into the client's world of thoughts, meanings and feelings. Empathy is an expression of the regard and respect the counsellor holds for the client whose frame of reference (their values, thoughts, meanings, feelings, cultural influences, experiences and perceptions) could be quite different from that of the counsellor. It's crucial that counsellors don't lose themselves in their client's material and that they retain their own sense of self.

The client needs to feel 'held' as well as understood. True empathic responding does both.

Empathic responding circumnavigates all the other skills. The ability to empathize with the other person is enhanced by an ever-alert attentiveness to facial expressions, **body language**, gestures and so on, and not only to what is being openly conveyed but also to the underlying implications. Intuition or 'hunches' have a part to play in empathic responding.

### Empathy and sympathy

Empathy is sometimes confused with sympathy. When we feel sympathy for someone we view them with pity: 'Poor Jennifer – she really can't cope now Harry has left her.' Pity is often linked with victimhood. While pity makes a victim of the sufferer, empathy empowers them; it says: 'I have a sense of your world – you're not alone, we'll go through this together.' The other person becomes an important subject of our interest rather than someone whose problems are far removed from our own experiences. We can tell we're objectifying someone when in our minds we slot them into a sociological category or stereotype like 'the abandoned wife', 'the single parent' or the adolescent 'delinquent'. Classifications like these can limit empathic understanding of people as individuals.

## _Awareness of body language_

Our inner emotional state is communicated through our bodies. We give each other messages through body movement, the intonation of our voice, facial expressions, posture, gestures and eye contact. Some of these movements might be slight or fleeting but in the heightened atmosphere of one-to-one counselling they are more often than not registered. When we counsel others we need to be aware of two sets of body language, our own and that of the client. As a helper our body needs to demonstrate behaviour that's facilitative.

## Posture

Our posture reveals the degree of interest we have in the client. When we sit back, away from the other person, we might seem to distance ourselves from them; and when we lean towards them we engage and show interest. Similarly, when we cross our arms and legs we convey the message that we are less open to the other person; that we're in some way protecting ourselves by closing off. In contrast, a relaxed and attentive posture tells the client that we're comfortable with ourselves and with them in the helping process. Although it would be unnatural to sit totally still throughout, too much shifting around can be distracting.

## The tone of voice

The tone of our voice also acts as an indicator of our thoughts and attitudes. If we speak too quietly or hesitantly the other person could find it hard to have confidence in us as a helper. It would be counter-productive to be too forceful or bombastic in the way we interact. If we talk clearly at a fairly steady level rather than sounding rushed or excited, and without mumbling or stumbling over our words, then we're probably getting it right. Sometimes it's appropriate to mirror the tone of the client's voice to help them hear the emotion conveyed.

## Words and body language

Words can be either congruent or incongruent with what our body is demonstrating. For example, we might say 'I understand' while looking perplexed, or say 'No, that doesn't shock me' having raised our eyebrows and crossed our arms and legs. What the body's doing is an indicator of deeper, sometimes unconscious feelings. A common display of incongruence is: when a client says they're angry while smiling, or that they're deeply sad but show little emotion. This can tell us that the client isn't comfortable in expressing their true emotions.

## The client's body language

While we, the counsellor or helper, need to be aware of our body language, it's also our work to decode, understand and interpret the body language of our client. What might their body language tell us? Body and facial expression can inform us about hidden feelings.

## *Reflecting skills*

Paraphrasing, summarizing and mirroring are ways of reflecting back the client's thoughts and feelings. They're methods of reiterating client expression in order that:

* the client can (re)hear what they've said
* the client gets a sense of themselves, i.e. how they're expressing themselves – as if a mirror were being held up to them
* the counsellor checks that what they're understanding (meanings, thoughts and feelings) is correct
* there's clarification of certain points (without asking intrusive questions)
* the material is made more 'manageable' for both counsellor and client
* there's ongoing communication between counsellor and client
* threads (of what the client has said) can be joined together to make a more coherent whole.

### Paraphrasing

Paraphrasing involves reflecting back the content and feelings of what the client is saying by drawing out the salient parts. Usually the content is repeated in the counsellor's own words, which gives a slightly different perspective on the material. Paraphrasing is best used at natural intervals or when it seems appropriate to reiterate what is being conveyed. It lets the client know that you are following what they say, that you're attentive to their personal details and understanding of their feelings and meanings.

## Mirroring

Mirroring bears a resemblance to parroting and has to be used with sensitivity to be well received by, and useful, to the client. The counsellor mirrors by, for example, repeating a line a client has said or mirroring an expression (take care that this is not straight mimicking – it should be subtle). A client might say, 'I'm enjoying my new job, it's a big challenge but I like challenges most of the time,' with a grimace at the end of the statement. You might have noticed that he seems to have mixed feelings about his new job and is perhaps wondering if he has made the right decision in accepting it or doubting that he is up to it. To check this out you could subtly mirror the grimace and pick up on his words: 'Most of the time...' This could help him get in touch with what's worrying him; it might be another challenge in his life that he hasn't yet mentioned.

## Summarizing

Summarizing is similar to paraphrasing, but it means putting together larger chunks of information when a client has talked for a length of time. While paraphrasing is relevant to one statement of whatever length, summarizing puts together a few or many. It's a way of keeping contact with a client, showing that you're following what they're saying and that you have an understanding of their underlying feelings. Another purpose of summarizing is that it brings together different threads of what has been expressed, providing an overview that enables the client to make connections and reach new insights into their problems. It's especially important when summarizing a lot of received information to finish with an enquiry about the accuracy of your understanding. You can check this out by saying, 'Is that what you feel?' or 'Does that sum it up?' or simply 'Am I getting this right?' Otherwise you might be going off on an agenda of your own.

## Minimal responses

Minimal responses are made to demonstrate the counsellor's attentiveness and understanding of what is said and also to encourage the client to continue. Minimal encouragements convey interest. Minimal responses include:

* 'mm', 'uh-huh'
* nodding
* using one word such as 'so', 'and', 'then'
* repeating one or a few key words the client has used.

## Words

People use specific words to communicate inner emotions. It's more difficult to say to someone, 'I completely lost control and I was destructive in the way I behaved' than 'I was in a rage.' The word 'rage' says a lot more than 'angry'; the word 'joy' is more revealing than 'happy'; the word 'morose' more specific than 'sad' or 'depressed'; the word 'devastated' more emotionally packed than 'hurt' and so on.

A word of caution — inevitably, it can happen that counsellors have a different understanding of a particular word or phrase from the client, so check that your understanding corresponds with the client's meaning.

## Silences

Managing silence can be difficult for the inexperienced counsellor, yet silences can be very productive. It can take some time to feel comfortable with silences. Ask yourself the following questions:

* How comfortable am I with silences?
* How often do I spend time by myself in silence?
* What associations do I have with silence?

Allowing silences gives the client space to reflect. As a new counsellor you might experience awkwardness at handling a silence but your threshold of silence will increase with experience and you'll be able to discern between different types. Sometimes clients are nervous, especially in the first or second session, and a protracted silence can be excruciatingly uncomfortable for them. If this happens it's advisable to acknowledge the rising discomfort by saying something like, 'I imagine it's difficult for you to be here' or ask, 'Are you feeling uncomfortable?' This will serve two purposes. First, it will break an uncomfortable silence and, second, it's likely to lead to disclosure of feelings. Clients can get lost in their own thoughts and feelings or feel overawed by them, and a silence can then occur. A summary of what you have understood could be useful at such a time. Sometimes a silence begins because the client is hoping for something from the counsellor; this might be reassurance or confirmation that the counsellor has been listening, or has understood what has been said.

# 4

# *the benefits of acquiring counselling skills*

Counselling skills, especially the 'core conditions' of empathy, congruence and genuineness, and unconditional positive regard, are applicable not only in the therapy room but also in personal relationships and a host of other workplace settings – the school, doctor's surgery and in probation work, for example. An individual's problems or anxieties can quite often relate to a specific area of their life; their health, for example, or academic attainment, and it can be extremely useful for practitioners in a wide range of fields to have acquired some degree of counselling skills. The secondary school, for instance, can be an especially fraught environment (for both pupils and teachers) and the promotion of the Rogerian core conditions can be extremely useful in creating a fruitful, happy learning environment – for both individual students and the school community as a whole.

The acquisition of counselling skills is empowering. It can help us gain insight into other people's behaviour as well as our own. Shakespeare described human relationships as a 'tangled web'. They're not always easy and yet they're the main source of human fulfilment – in marriage, partnership, family life, community life and work. Lack of communication is often cited as the reason why relationships break down. Without the tools of good communication we're apt to respond defensively when, for example, others are angry with us. We feel blamed and rush to our own defence without finding out the associated reasons and feelings of the other person. We take offence at each other's moods and actions if they're at odds with, or in some way exclude, our own. Also we might lose a sense of ourselves in relation to other people.

## How skills can be applied to personal and work situations

* Listen carefully and attentively, without being defensive or attacking.
* Use your powers of observation – notice the person's body language, appearance, gestures, posture, eye contact and tone of voice.
* Don't bombard the person with questions but do invite them to expand on things they say that seem important or if you don't understand something.
* Use questions to open out what the person is trying to convey and to expand your understanding of the other person's thoughts, feelings and meanings.
* Paraphrase (repeating, not verbatim but in your own words) to check and clarify the content of what's been said and the feelings behind it.
* Use minimal responses such as 'Yes', 'mm', 'uh-huh', nodding, etc. to demonstrate attention, to show you are following what's being said and to encourage further exploration.

* Summarize when the person has talked for a while. Keep track of and join together themes, to check you've understood what's been said and to help the person get an overall picture.
* Use immediacy to address 'here and now' issues in the relationship.
* Use confrontation tentatively – examine your motives, don't use it to accuse or humiliate; examine your own agenda and challenge the behaviour, not the person.

An appropriate time to use confrontation skills is when a person has become rude or angry towards others or is repeatedly demonstrating destructive behaviour. At work it might be necessary to confront an employee who is continually late, or at school a pupil who is bullying other children. Remember the aim of the confrontation. Is it intended to achieve a greater understanding of the problems? Be aware of whose needs are being met by the confrontation. Do you need to express your own frustration, irritability or stress? If so, it could be more productive to use immediacy skills to address what's happening between the two of you. Be 'real' yourself. Tell the other person about your feelings if they're conflicting; say, for instance, 'I would like to help but I'm frightened/angry/upset' but convey this in a way that's not dismissive or rejecting of the other person.

## Applying the core conditions of person-centred therapy

Using the example of Colin from Chapter 1, imagine what the response might be if he told a friend or a member of his family about his feelings of hopelessness.

Let's suppose that Colin's friend responded to his depression by saying, 'I felt like that when I lost my job but something will turn up, you'll see,' or, 'Come on, it's not as bad as it seems. Have a drink, that'll cheer you up. This isn't like you.' Colin's friend is trying to do what comes automatically to most people; he tries to cheer Colin up to take his mind off his problems when staying with his feelings could prove more helpful for him. While the friend's responses intend to reassure, they're likely to have the opposite effect. The solutions offered represent his inability and unwillingness to investigate Colin's predicament any further.

Colin's wife might say: 'Pull yourself together; look at the effect you're having on your family. I don't know what's got into you, you're just feeling sorry for yourself. You have responsibilities to face up to – you're being pathetic. I've got problems too, but I have to get on with things.' This response is more condemnatory than the last example. Living with Colin, she's more involved on a daily basis than his friend is. She's becoming increasingly critical of him because he appears to be rejecting her and the life they have led and she feels afraid. Her way of dealing with Colin's depression is to withdraw her affection from him, which leaves him feeling more desolate and unlovable in his present emotional state.

The telling question is: Were Colin's friend and wife showing signs of encouraging him to talk and were they really listening to him? Let's look at how the core conditions of Rogerian person-centred therapy might be applied.

### Unconditional positive regard

What can unconditional positive regard mean in relation to Colin, his family and friends, and their largely subjective responses to his anguish? Do they respect him? They would probably argue that they both love and respect him. But the key point is whether they are able to demonstrate that they fully accept him when he's in crisis and needs their understanding. Using the short description of their responses as representing their general attitude to Colin's problems, we can appreciate that he needs some help rather than cheering up or being ridiculed. It would help if people close to him could:

* respect his right to express his emotions
* accept different aspects of his personality – some positive, some negative
* respect his right to have different values from theirs
* respect his right to self-exploration and self-discovery
* accept his right to change.

They need to be able to be objective, accept what Colin is saying, without blocking out or censoring the painful truth of his situation. Colin's wife and friend might think that what they're saying to him will help but:

* Are they adopting a non-judgemental stance?
* Are they accepting his vulnerability?
* Are they able to see beyond their own requirements of him?

## Congruence and genuineness

Being congruent is when a person is fully genuine and not hiding behind a front. They're being honest about their own feelings and being open to the other person. So would you say that Colin's wife and friend are being honest and open with him? For example:

* Are they sharing their real feelings with him? – perhaps fear, inadequacy, anger or pity.
* Are they affirming that they hear what he's saying?
* Are they able to admit that they don't have the solutions?
* Are they willing to enter the struggle with him – rather than retreating into the safety of 'quick fix' answers?

## Empathy

Would you say that Colin's wife and friend are empathic in their responses? Are they showing him that they are willing to enter into his experience with him as if they were experiencing the same, effectively walking in his shoes? Empathic response would mean that:

* they really listen to him
* they focus on Colin's thoughts and feelings
* they're able to put their own requirements and problems aside
* they're able to be involved in what he is going through without getting totally lost in the process
* they can differentiate between Colin's and their own feelings (fear, pain, loss, etc.).

By acquiring counselling skills you won't become a counsellor *per se*. However, by learning how to use some of the skills and by familiarizing yourself with core conditions you can enhance the relationships in your life, helping you to acknowledge and understand both other people's feelings and your own.

Had Colin's wife and friend had knowledge of certain skills, they could have responded differently. They could have listened actively and adopted the values of respect, genuineness, empathy and acceptance. They would have been able to own their feelings and avoid projecting their anxieties back on to Colin.

## Uses of counselling skills in work settings

Many people benefit from the use of counselling skills in their jobs. Those who work in the caring professions – such as nurses and social workers – might have had relevant skills included in their training. Those in any job that involves interaction with other people could benefit from learning counselling skills, including those working in large corporate companies in personnel departments and managerial roles. With this in mind, let's look briefly at a few examples of how people can and do use skills and adopt core values at work. In the main example I draw on my own experiences of working in groups with young people in a school environment.

### Teachers and counselling skills

It's widely recognized that teachers play an enormously important role in a young person's life. Between the ages of 5 and 16 years or older, children spend more weekday hours in the school environment with teachers than they do with their parents.

Inevitably, some children have difficulties which may relate to their home life, peer group pressures, schoolwork or slotting into the school environment. Counselling skills can help the teacher communicate empathetically and effectively with a child who is in trouble in some way.

Teachers realize that a happy, well-adjusted child tends to work more productively, both separately and with others. I use 'well-adjusted' here to mean a child who has self-esteem and a strong enough sense of self (what Freud termed 'Ego strength') to engage with others within the school environment. At a counselling agency where I initially trained, there was a high proportion of teachers among the trainees. They recognized that at times their pupils needed emotional support that they would try to give but sometimes felt unable to do this satisfactorily.

A child might be quiet, withdrawn or sullen, increasingly miss school, and never get homework or projects in on time. They're likely to feel the wrath of a teacher when clearly they need help. The teacher, too, is likely to be stressed, overworked and exasperated by the individual needs of this troublesome child. The child is **acting out** – their behaviour is saying that there could be something drastically wrong in their life and they're not coping.

In this type of situation communication can break down rapidly. The child is in deep water. Punitive measures serve only to alienate them further. It becomes a pupil versus teacher and school situation, and the problem can escalate. Sometimes the child is eventually excluded from school. The resources needed to educate expelled children can be enormous, and these resources could have been placed within the school setting at the onset of problems. Ideally, schools would have a resident counsellor who would provide troubled pupils with individual support, support that says: 'We appreciate that something is wrong in your world, we want to understand and help you. To do this we'll set time aside to spend with you, to look at your needs one to one – you're worth that attention.' Unfortunately having a counsellor as a member of staff isn't usually regarded as a necessity and lack of funds is often cited as the reason.

Clearly it's in the interests of both pupils and teachers that pupils are able to address their feelings within the school environment. This calls for clear boundaries. It wouldn't be in the interest of the smooth running of a school to have a riot of unleashed emotions. If dissatisfactions and problems are to be held and contained, there needs to be a place to register them before they escalate into something less manageable – this could be the school counsellor or it could be a skilled, empathic teacher who is capable of putting counselling skills to use.

Good teaching can instil a sense of self-worth in a child, not only by encouraging academic achievement but also by teaching children to value themselves and other people. To make this possible they need to feel that they're (most of the time at least) accepted and valued by others and that they have a part to play as individuals.

If a teacher is able to use the core conditions and is familiar with various counselling skills, then they can put these to use in various contexts – in a one-to-one relationship with a child or young person who is demonstrating antisocial behaviour and also in relation to the class as a whole, in the understanding and management of group dynamics.

## Doctors and counselling skills

A doctor told me that he had undertaken brief counselling training because he was increasingly dissatisfied with his lack of ability to be fully attentive of his patients. He realized that many of his patients needed to feel that they were being listened to and responded to as if they were important. He appreciated that his manner was not conveying his genuine concern.

He considers that the counselling skills he has acquired have helped him to look more deeply at the patient as an individual. Subsequently he's more inclined to suggest that a patient who is suffering from depression has counselling or psychotherapy than to prescribe antidepressants automatically – he now prescribes these less frequently. He told me that he's more likely than before to ask depressed patients, and patients who have persistent symptoms that resist medication, open questions about what's going on in their lives and their relationships with significant others as a means of assessing appropriate treatment.

# Probation officers and counselling skills

I asked an ex-colleague of mine who had trained and worked as a counsellor how she uses her skills in her new career as a probation officer. She said that the skills she learned are of great value to her. She can engage with her clients (young offenders) on an empathic level, appreciating the whole person. She's more likely to make links between the offender's crimes and their past childhood, which helps her to write pre-sentencing reports. In these she might comment on events in the offender's childhood that she considers to have had a contributing effect, resulting in poor self-esteem and an inability to handle difficulties. She stressed that this in no way makes her a 'soft touch'. The counselling skills help her to challenge effectively, in an unthreatening manner. This might include challenging the offender's attitude towards issues of power and control. Having the skills also helps her to recognize certain patterns of behaviour. She commented:

> *Sometimes a persistent offender enjoys having a problem in the sense that it in some way defines him. He becomes caught up in a cycle of repetition of events. By tentative challenging I can bring issues into the open. In this way he can choose to own his behaviour and make some sense of it.*

The knowledge and practice of listening and responding skills can give us more choice about how to deal with some stresses in the work environment. It's important, when we use counselling skills, that we're aware of our limitations as helpers, recognizing when we're perhaps out of our depth and when it's time to refer a person to someone with appropriate training and experience — otherwise there can be a conflict of roles. The objective isn't to overload ourselves with responsibilities but instead to lighten our load by improving our relationships with those around us.

# 5

# *course components*

Professional counselling is rooted in solid, thorough training, often taking the form of foundational training then a diploma course that is likely to be two or three years part-time (perhaps one day a week). Key components of every counselling course include learning theory, acquiring skills, practising skills with other trainees as well as with 'outside' clients, assignments, ongoing assessment and possibly a final written exam and/or viva. Practice and supervision are likely to be at the heart of the course: the role-play session featuring 'counsellor', 'client' and 'observer' is the classic applied technique.

All counselling courses emphasize the importance of the trainees' own personal growth and self-awareness and for this reason such courses can often prove very emotional and challenging for participants. The often high financial cost of such courses is another factor to be taken into account, although grants and sponsorship may be available.

# Background

Counselling started becoming professionalized in countries like Australia, New Zealand and Great Britain in the late 1960s and early 1970s, when training courses in counselling were offered for the first time. This followed a precedent set in the USA in the 1950s by the work of Carl Rogers and his contemporaries. Originally a person training to become a psychoanalyst would undergo personal analysis for a considerable time. Receiving analysis from senior analysts was at the time the only method of becoming familiar with the workings of psychoanalysis. It was the responsibility of the training analyst to decide whether or not the candidate was suitable material to become an analyst.

Gradually other methods of teaching and learning were added as the canon of analytical literature grew; case discussions were opened out to include analysts in training and theoretical seminars were introduced. It was the humanistic therapists, with their emphasis on the experiential, who introduced innovative ideas about therapy and, with these, new training methods evolved. In the 1940s and 1950s Carl Rogers and his associates experimented with different training techniques in client-centred therapy, and some are still in use – notably students watching and commenting on films of counselling sessions, students as co-therapists in sessions, personal growth groups, and peer and self-assessments.

Counselling training has become highly structured and systematized, especially in an academic setting. Training courses are thriving and are today available in a variety of forms in universities, colleges, training institutes and agencies in many parts of the world.

# Choosing a course

Professional associations offer accreditation to courses that meet their standards and this is worth keeping in mind when you select your course. Courses on offer range from non-certificated starter courses at basic skills level to diplomas, Masters degrees and PhDs. Counselling has become highly professionalized, especially in the USA. People do practise without professional credentials, considering themselves to be counsellors, but this is generally frowned upon by qualified practitioners and professional organizations alike because the ethical standards and the integrity of the unqualified practitioner go unmonitored.

Courses can be very expensive, and the cost of the personal therapy, usually a condition of the professional course, adds to the expense. Over a period of usually two or three years the total can seem extortionate and a criticism of counsellor training systems is that it's only the financially solvent – and that usually means middle-class people – who can afford to undertake training. However, financially disadvantaged people are usually eligible for help with fees/books. Some universities and colleges offer reduced fees for those on state benefits and candidates can apply to charities and organizations that offer funding.

A diploma course in counselling, geared to a professional standard, usually comprises of a foundation year, which might be certificated as a first stage, followed by a further two years. The complete training is likely to take three years part-time – possibly one day per week, although some courses entail weekend and week blocks of training. Before being accepted on a reputable course that leads to a professional qualification, you'll be required to have training and/or experience relevant to the level you are hoping to enter. For example, a Diploma in Counselling course might require a candidate to have completed a certain number of hours' training through previous courses and/or to have had relevant experience working in a counselling capacity with an agency.

Joining an agency that offers counselling is probably the best way to begin because of the training they offer, the availability of clients to work with and the back-up of close supervision. Established agencies or organizations usually work to ethical standards specified by a professional (overseeing) association, and they therefore have professional accountability through membership. At least some of the staff members will be accredited by a professional organization.

# _Acquiring skills_

Skills practice forms an important part of the majority of counselling training courses. A basic skills course would contain mainly skills learning and practice, including a familiarization with Rogerian core conditions.

## Methods commonly used in the teaching/learning of skills

* Video demonstrations of 'expertise' in skill
* Practice in triads of 'counsellor', 'client' and 'observer'
* Brainstorming
* Class handout examples of 'positive' and 'negative' use of skills
* Video recordings, taken while practising the skills in triads, using role play or personal material
* Performance feedback given by tutors and others.

The aim of familiarizing the trainee counsellor with these skills is to widen their repertoire of responses to client material and help them to discriminate between effective and ineffective ways of communicating or intervening. The minimum requirements for a competent counsellor are that they have a workable knowledge of theoretical models, a range of skills, and have developed self-awareness.

## Practising with others

During the training you'll be practising the skills with other trainees – with a partner or others, using role play or personal material. Role play is what happens when the person acting the part of the client adopts a role and set of problematic circumstances to present to the person acting as the counsellor. The client has the script of the role they adopt to work from. The person playing the role can develop the character, improvising details that will enhance understanding of the 'story'. The words 'acting', 'improvising' and 'script' may suggest something akin to amateur dramatics, which might seem daunting to the person who is the client. Don't worry; good acting ability is not necessary. Role play is more a matter of entering into the set of circumstances – rather like the practice of empathy. The brief script you will read prior to taking on a persona is a guideline or baseline story and you'll inevitably bring parts of your own life experience to the part. The counsellor's knowledge is limited to a few brief facts, enough to give them the bones, to which the client adds meat with the help of the counsellor's interventions. This triad formation, when one person acts as counsellor, another as the client and the third person as the observer, is an ideal format for skills practice. Individual skills can be practised by focusing on one area at a time, such as: empathy, paraphrasing, questions, summarizing and so on.

The role of the observer is to watch over the interaction between counsellor and client, either writing notes or making mental notes with regard to the exchange. The observer notes the whole content of the session: the process, what happens, how, why, when, silences, awkwardness and so on, and the body language of the two participants.

When an exercise is finished the observer comments – that is, gives feedback – on the ways the counsellor helped (or didn't help) the client to explore issues generally, and also on how they met the criteria of specific tasks set by the exercise.

## Feedback

The benefit of working with other trainees is that you can give and receive feedback. Feedback is information given to us by other people about our counselling skills practice. It's potentially a valuable learning tool. The use of feedback requires a specific approach if it's not to become open to abuse or sycophantic appraisal. It requires honesty, self-scrutiny and humility. It's not easy for any of us to have weaknesses pointed out and feedback needs to be given sensitively. Feedback can also be affirming when our strengths are highlighted. It's invaluable in helping us identify our strengths and weaknesses in the way we apply the various skills.

# Developing self-awareness

## Groupwork

Working in groups is commonly used as a method of developing self-awareness and interpersonal skills. As we have seen, the small group is used in the development of supervision skills, offering feedback and insight relating to each other's work with clients. Other groupwork is concerned with personal development and group processes. The key word to sum up the purpose of groupwork is 'insight'. Experiencing oneself with and separate from others in a group is a learning process *par excellence*, likely to stir up complex, ambivalent, primary feelings such as rivalry between members, a need to merge with others, a need to assert one's own individuality, projections on to others (what can't be personally owned) and fantasies about self and other group members. The facilitator or conductor offers interpretations of content and feelings of the group.

**Positive experiences from groupwork**

*   Participants feel valued by others.
*   Participants feel supported by others. They give and receive mirroring.
*   Members engage in a process of identification and empathy to help them resolve their own conflicts.
*   Deeper levels of communication are reached – in a therapeutic context, things that couldn't be communicated previously can now be shared.
*   Builds trust, confidence, affirmation of self.
*   Helps individuals to re-own 'split off' parts of themselves.
*   Stronger understanding of self in relation to others.
*   Understanding of unconscious processes of groups and social situations.

# Supervision

During training the trainee is given supervision by either a course tutor or an outside supervisor (i.e. someone who comes in to carry out the task). Peer supervision is often a feature of diploma-level courses, where the trainees learn the skills of supervision by observing the tutor at work and by practising under the watchful eye and listening ear of the tutor/supervisor.

Supervision always plays an important, supportive part of a counsellor's work. It's a 'sounding board', a safety net and a method of learning from a therapist who usually has more training and experience than the counsellors they're supervising.

Proficient supervision gives the trainee counsellor room to 'move around' the client, helping them to understand the client from different angles. The following are ways the supervisor assists:

* As a safety net for the counsellor they offer support and protection.
* As a third party they offer another perspective – a new insight, the 'aha' factor. The supervisor might, for example, use symbolism or imagery to extend understanding.
* To help the counsellor explore transference and countertransference.
* To monitor the counsellor's work – e.g. check that they're working in an appropriate way with the client (that is, within ethical standards), including an exploration of theory and techniques being used.
* As 'outside' observers they can see blind spots and help the counsellor to explore 'stuckness'.
* To explore the client-counsellor relationship – 'the working alliance'.
* To help with planning and structuring – questions such as 'Where are you going with this?' assist in clarification.

It's a requirement of professional associations that to qualify for accreditation, a counsellor must have regular supervision from an appropriately qualified supervisor. (Supervisors check that counsellors work within a code of ethics and code of practice.) The association will stipulate the ratio of hours of counselling to hours spent with a supervisor (e.g. four hours or four 50-minute sessions of counselling require one hour of supervision). Professional associations are very helpful with enquiries and are often an excellent source of information and resources.

### Group supervision

Group supervision is sometimes a practical option for small agencies and is a common component of training courses. Peer supervision means a small group of counsellor trainees acting as supervisors for each other, usually with a tutor as the main supervisor and overseer of proceedings. Client casework is presented in the session and the trainee counsellor who's presenting client material in supervision gives the other members of the group written relevant details, including: agency setting, contract, client details (the client's real identity is protected by using their initials only or a pseudonym), history, family relationships, presenting problems, current issues, what's happening in the counselling process and theory referred to. The trainee also gives an informal oral presentation of the client's case. When they've finished talking through the case history of the client to the others, the other members then give their contribution, taking a supervisory role. This includes asking questions to help clarify details, challenging and offering observations with regard to relational elements, transference issues or incongruences in the presentation.

## _Theory and practice_

Part of the training will concentrate on the theoretical underpinnings, concepts, beliefs and aims of various approaches concerned with counselling. Developmental psychology, group theory and dynamics, mental health issues, ethics in counselling, bereavement, child abuse, aspects of sociology (class, race and cultural issues and gender issues) are all probable additional topics. Lengthy booklists are given out. The student needs to know and understand theory as well as how to apply it.

With this in mind, theory periods usually involve lectures given by tutors, followed by questions and forms of practice, such as small-group discussion, brainstorming or exchanges of ideas and experiences (at times writing these down on flipchart paper). For instance, following a lecture on gender issues a large group of 20 or more trainees might be asked by a tutor to form smaller groups containing four people in each, providing a 'safer', more intimate environment to address questions for discussion.

This kind of exercise develops self-awareness, crucial to counselling other people. Knowledge of theory and how the trainee is applying it is also explored within supervision sessions and in assignments.

## *Personal therapy*

Personal therapy is also commonly a compulsory element of the training of a professional counsellor. Personal therapy enhances understanding by:

* Developing an ability to separate own material from that of the client – i.e. dealing with unresolved personal conflicts.
* Learning from the counsellor/therapist subliminally, taking in how they are working/relating.
* Being a client, building an understanding of what it feels like to be a client – e.g. vulnerable, apprehensive, dependent, trusting.
* Giving experience of the processes and the stages of counselling – e.g. beginnings, endings, transference, resistance.
* Deepening self-understanding of own personal issues, making links with childhood experiences and 'stuck' patterns of relating to others, through transference, exploring personal defences, resistances.

## *Exams and ongoing assessment*

It's worth considering what methods are used to assess learning on a course that interests you. Some people find exams a terrible pressure, while others prefer them to extensive ongoing assessments. Written theory-based exams may be set at the end of each year. Some courses are more academic than others; some require the implementation of research methods, for example. Most commonly, testing procedures involve skills observation, written assignments, peer, tutor and self-assessments, and written exams or vivas.

An educational institution uses assessment to gauge whether an individual has reached the necessary standard in the work, either to move on to the next stage or for the attainment of an award. Assessments are both summative, to assess the point a student has reached, and formative, helping in the development of an allotted task or goal. Assessment is an ongoing process where tutors, in a teaching role or as facilitators, are continually observing and noting the trainee's work in various learning situations; for example, via role play or using personal issues in skills practice, in supervision groups, personal development groups or interpersonal groups, and in the contributions made in theory, learning and discussions. It's common practice to use a combination of tutor, peer and self-assessment at a culmination point of learning skills or theory. For example, the first year of a counselling training course might concentrate on skills practice, and at the end of the year students are assessed on their level of competence in using the skills. Feedback is usually given both orally and in written form. Peer assessments of an individual's ability to use various skills will be based on observation of the person counselling others and the personal experience of being counselled by the candidate in the triad format of skills practice. The individual student might also be asked to assess their own abilities, highlighting strong and weaker aspects of what they have learned.

Written assignments are another method used by tutors/trainers to assess the learning of skills and theoretical perspectives. In academic settings and in training institutes alike, students are usually asked to produce a minimum of two or three essays per year, of 2,000–3,000 words, and a dissertation or project at the end of the last year of the course. The student is most likely to be asked to choose a topic for the dissertation that reflects the learning accumulated from the course and that has relevance for their client group.

## Vivas

A viva usually combines oral and written elements, an audio or video recording accompanied by a verbatim transcript of a section of the recorded session. Typically a viva will take the form of questions and discussion around the presented case material. Usually the counsellor in training makes, with the permission of the client – and, when working with an agency, the agency's approval – a few recordings of a counselling session and one recording is chosen for the viva presentation. The recording doesn't have to be technically perfect but is chosen to reflect use of theory, skills, awareness of the counselling process and so on.

## Professional considerations

Towards the end of your course, as you focus on the professional work you might undertake, your attention could be drawn once more to ethical issues and practice. National professional organizations publish copies of their code of ethics and practice for counsellors, which provide a guideline for professional use. A code of ethics is likely to encompass values, responsibility, anti-discriminatory practice, confidentiality, contracts, boundaries and competence. Members of professional associations are required to abide by existing codes that provide a common frame of reference; they clarify counsellor's responsibilities towards clients, colleagues and the community at large.

A code of ethics is translated into a code of practice that applies guideline principles to the counselling situation. The code of practice is likely to be concerned with issues including: client safety, counsellor responsibility and accountability, clear contracting and counsellor competence. Professional indemnity insurance, recommended by professional associations, is another safeguard to be considered. It's worth noting that while counselling for an agency the counsellor is offered protection under the agency's insurance cover. Working to ethical standards, acquiring insurance and having adequate supervision become fully the responsibility of the counsellor when they practise privately.

Another consideration, at the conclusion of a course, is further follow-up training; for example, in a specialist area such as family therapy, or in supervision and training, or in attaining a higher level of qualification such as a Masters degree or PhD.

# 6

# *the psychoanalytic psychodynamic approach*

The psychoanalytic, humanistic and behavioural models of therapy form the foundations of all other kinds of psychotherapy. In counselling, the psychoanalytic approach is represented by psychodynamic models. Humanistic approaches include person-centred therapy, Gestalt therapy and transactional analysis. The behavioural approaches include cognitive behavioural therapy (CBT) and rational emotive therapy (RET). Although the core approaches are fundamentally different – the psychodynamic places emphasis on unconscious processes and transference; the humanistic on the relationship between client and counsellor and the concept of self-actualization; and the behavioural on monitoring and changing the individual's thoughts and behaviours – they have proved to be complementary to each other. Many counselling training courses integrate elements of all three models.

In this chapter we explore the psychodynamic models set out by thinkers such as Sigmund Freud and Carl Jung, whose contributions revolutionized the treatment of psychiatric disorders at the turn of the twentieth century.

## Origins

The psychodynamic approach has direct links with Freudian psychoanalysis. Sigmund Freud's theories (see Ruth Snowden's *Freud – The Key Ideas*) have been developed, modified and adapted by different strands of psychodynamic theorists. Many of Freud's original concepts remain central to this approach: for example, his theories of the unconscious, transference and countertransference; the importance of formative childhood experiences and relationships; and the use of dreams and metaphor as means of understanding the human psyche. These are among the tools used in the work of the psychodynamic counsellor. We can understand the term 'psychodynamic' by dividing it into its two parts. The first part derives from the Greek root word *psyche* and, in relation to therapy, refers to the tripart combination of the mind, emotions and spirit or soul. The word 'dynamic' refers to the constant interaction and movement between these three forces both internally (within ourselves) and externally in relation to other people and our environment.

## The unconscious

Freud was fascinated by material that he believed lay hidden in the human psyche. He identified three categories of mental process:

1 The conscious – material (facts, feelings and thoughts) that the patient is aware of in the present.
2 The preconscious – material (ideas and memories) that are not conscious but are easily accessed.
3 The unconscious – material (desires or impulses) that lie hidden, buried from the conscious mind.

Freud later identified three driving forces of the mind.

### The Id (It)

The Id is the part of the unconscious mind that contains the instinctual drives and impulses that motivate our behaviour.

The primitive impulses driven by our instinctual needs are at odds with the Ego and the Superego. Both of these parts of the unconscious temper the basic drives of the Id. We might, for example, take a strong dislike towards someone; the Id would tell us to harm them or get rid of them in some way while the other parts of our unconscious mind would apply reasoning to the situation. The Id can be thought of as the child part of the unconscious. Because it forms the underlying motivations and drives of our actions, it's our spontaneous 'dangerous' side that wishes to follow the 'pleasure principle'. The Id might say: 'This is what I want, what I really really want.'

## The Ego (I)

The Ego is the rational, partly conscious part of the mind that makes decisions and copes with the external world. The Ego says: 'I am, I can and I will.' The Ego can be related to the more grown-up side of our mind; it takes care of us, telling us we are doing OK. The Ego facilitates mediation with others and adaptation to our environment.

## The Superego (higher I)

The Superego is the 'conscientious' side of our mind. It contains internalized societal and parental rules and taboos. As we take these into our unconscious mind, the taboos are translated into 'I should', 'I ought' and 'I must'. The Superego is the source of guilt and ideals. Both the Superego and the Id are largely unconscious.

The role of the analyst was to assist the patient (as they were then termed) in translating unconscious material into conscious understanding. Using hypnosis in treatment, Freud's attention was drawn to the workings of the unconscious mind. An aim was to give the patient insight into areas of their psyche where they had 'stored' an experience that had been too painful or threatening for them to acknowledge fully at the time. These remained in the unconscious mind as repressed memories, causing disturbance in the patient's vital functioning. Freud believed that when patients were freed of these experiences, and the accompanying emotions that debilitated them, they would be more in control of their emotions and be happier.

Freud considered that the source of neuroses could always be traced back to early childhood, although the symptoms of the neurotic conflict could manifest at a later stage. 'Neurosis' (or disturbance), lying dormant in the unconscious mind, could cause strong irrational reactions in later life. An example of this is demonstrated in our anxious responses towards other people.

Freud noted that people repeatedly replay difficult or troubling relationships and situations that were originally experienced in the early years of life. The individual will have the 'compulsion to repeat' the unresolved material, until the unconscious element is brought into consciousness.

## Developmental psychology

Psychodynamic theories regard the child's early environment as important and for this reason a psychodynamic training involves the study of developmental psychology. Psychoanalysts, beginning with Freud himself, have formed theories of human developmental stages.

### The developmental stages delineated by Sigmund Freud

The early writings of Freud divide the human developmental stages into three: oral, anal and sexual.

1 Oral, 0–2 years: At this stage the infant experiences pleasure through the mouth, mainly through gratification from sucking, so toys and other objects are put into the mouth and 'felt' by the mouth.

2 Anal, 2–4 years: At this stage of development the child takes a sensual interest in their own faeces, experiencing a gratification in a substance that they produce. This can result in the child experimenting with smearing or eating or withholding faeces as a means of control.

**3** Phallic, 4–7 years: The Superego develops within this age range as the focus of interest moves from the anus to the genitals as a focus of gratification. The parents become models for role identification. The Oedipus complex occurs during the phallic stage.

## The Oedipus complex

The term Oedipus complex derives its name from the mythical (Greek) figure of Oedipus, who unwittingly killed his father and married his mother. The Oedipus complex is a collection of unconscious desires to 'possess' the parent of the opposite sex and 'eliminate' the parent of the same sex. The Oedipal stage occurs between the ages of three and six and, according to traditional Freudian views, is a universal component of development.

Freud said, 'A child's first choice of an object is an incestuous one' and 'Incestuous wishes are a primordial human heritage. The Oedipal complex (phallic stage) is the central phenomenon of the sexual period of early childhood.' With its dissolution, it submits to repression and is followed by what Freud called the **latency period**. Disintegration occurs for a number of reasons, due to disappointments growing out of the hopeless longing for the parent who is fixated upon, or to a castration anxiety. Castration enters the boy child's imagination when he first views the genital region of the female child, noting the absence of a penis. The boy then believes that all women, including his mother, have been castrated.

The child's Ego turns from the Oedipus complex, replacing object cathexes (i.e. the investing of his libidinal sexual energy in the parent) with other identifications. The father's authority is at this time introjected into the Ego and forms the centre of the Superego. The position appropriates the prohibition against incest and rescues the Ego from the libidinal object cathexes. The Oedipus complex is thereby 'desexualised and sublimated', and the latency period begins.

## The Electra complex

The girl child also develops an Oedipus complex, which Freud initially termed the **Electra complex**. The girl's clitoris acts as a penis until she becomes aware that she has no penis and considers herself inferior, which results in 'penis envy'. At first she understands the lack as temporary, consoling herself with the belief that as she grows older she will acquire a penis; later, instead of making the connection between her lack of penis and sexual completion, she presumes castration has occurred. Freud wrote, 'The essential difference thus comes about that the girl accepts castration as an accomplished fact whereas the boy fears the possibility of its occurrence.'

The girl's Oedipus complex is a modified version of that of the boy, basically consisting of the girl's wish to take her mother's position in her father's affection and adopt a feminine attitude towards him. She attempts to compensate for the loss of a penis by desiring 'the gift' of bearing her father's child. The resolution of the Oedipus complex occurs because the wish remains unfulfilled. However, according to Freud, the two desires – to have a penis and a child – remain in the unconscious, preparing the female for her later sexual role.

## Latency stage

The latency stage is from six to puberty. The process that led to the dissolution of the Oedipus complex has saved the penis, but because its function has been compromised the latency period begins, interrupting the child's sexual development. Freud believed that if the Ego has repressed the complex, then the complex will persist in the unconscious within the Id and is likely, at some time, to result in 'pathogenic effect' (disturbance or disease). The genital stage, from puberty to adulthood, follows the latency stage.

Others who have contributed to developmental psychology and personality theories are Jean Piaget, whose concern was with a child's cognitive development, and the psychologist John Bowlby, who wrote studies of 'attachment behaviour' in relation to human psychological development.

## Jean Piaget's cognitive developmental stages

The Swiss developmental psychologist Jean Piaget was one of the first to study cognitive development in children, focusing on the importance of sensorimotor (sensory and motor mechanisms) and ideomotor (putting ideas into action) learning – the young child's developing ability to translate their perceptions into actions, organizing their thoughts into a series of actions. Within the sensorimotor (0–2 years) stage the infant develops an ability to interact with their environment through the senses. In Piagetian theory the preoperatory stage of cognitive development (2–7 years) follows the sensorimotor stage. The preoperatory stage is offset by the child's 'object concept' of 'object permanence', when the child becomes aware that physical objects are permanent and exist as a separate entity without their involvement in interaction. It's also the time when the child learns the use of a 'system of symbols' – words and language to relate to the world around – but at this stage the child's thought is intuitive rather than logical. The concrete operatory stage or level (7–12 years) represents a leap in cognitive abilities involving the use of logic to solve problems. By now the child can differentiate between ways of communicating and can cope with concrete situations.

Abstract reasoning comes into play in the formal operator level of cognition development (12 years to adulthood). Piaget called it 'the metaphysical age *par excellence*'. In the preadolescent to adolescent stage of development the young person gradually exercises their 'autonomous reasoning' to test the rules of society with a view to finding personal meaning.

## John Bowlby's attachment theory

The psychoanalyst John Bowlby, whose work has its roots in Melanie Klein's child development theory, wrote extensively on the theme of attachment with regard to loss, sadness and depression. Bowlby wrote *Attachment and Loss*, a three-volume exploration of attachment behaviour from an object relations perspective, identifying the early human need to maintain close contact with a parent or another significant person. A healthy 'secure attachment' develops when the individual, as an infant and young child, has consistency of care and feels confident and secure in parental availability (mainly that of the mother), having experienced her for the main part to be responsive, loving and safe. An 'anxious attachment' forms when a child has inconsistent 'mothering' or the loss of maternal, parental figures or significant other (a carer). Bowlby wrote that one of the typical patterns of pathogenic parenting was 'discontinuities of parenting'. The early unsatisfactory prototypal attachment relationship can affect the ability to form healthy attachments to others in later life.

## Object relations

The object relations theorists – Donald W. Winnicott, Ronald Fairbairn, Melanie Klein and others – also saw great significance in the child's first impression of the world. The object relations school moved away from the classical Freudian libidinal theories of instinctual pleasure-seeking drives, placing emphasis on human contact and relationships. The term 'object relations' refers to the central theme of the theory, which is that the baby's emotional well-being and development depends on certain relational needs being met. Melanie Klein, who's sometimes described as having bridged the gap between the object relations school and classic Freudian analysis, retained the idea of infantile instincts and drives as basic to the psyche, while introducing the concept of the infant as 'object seeking' as opposed to 'satisfaction seeking'. The infant's instinctive drive is both to survive and to satisfy their needs in relation to a loving, nurturing 'object' or person, usually the mother or a central figure.

The object relation theorists suggested that the mother's breast is an object of satisfaction and comfort that is not always available; therefore a 'transitional object' such as a dummy or a teddy bear is used as a temporary replacement. The 'good breast' and the 'bad breast' are terms used to describe the infant's impression of the breast as part object – as a potentially endless source of nourishment and pleasure it is a 'good object', and the frustrating breast that is taken away is a 'bad object'. Winnicott suggested that the child needs 'good enough mothering' – by which he meant a good enough facilitative environment to assist emotional and psychological development.

Klein, who regarded herself as a Freudian, believed that the first few weeks of a baby's life were significant. As a child analyst she used 'play analysis', using drawing and simple play materials and toys to help her understand the psychological world of the child. Winnicott also recommended that the counsellor let the client 'play' as a means of unravelling their story or rediscovering parts of themselves.

## *Transference and countertransference*

Transference was a term coined by Freud to describe a phenomenon he observed occurring between Josef Breuer, a colleague of Freud, and his patient Anna O., who became increasingly dependent on Breuer and fantasized that she was pregnant with his child. Freud was of the opinion that Anna (her real name was Bertha Pappenheim) had fallen in love with or become infatuated by her doctor, but that the manifest feelings really belonged to a relationship from her past and a resolution of the original disturbance would effect a 'cure'. In a paper entitled 'General Theory of the Neuroses' (1916–17) Freud wrote of transference as 'a newly created and transformed neurosis' that, within treatment, came to replace the original disturbance. He believed that the 'mastering' of the 'artificial neurosis', the transferred emotions, led to the elimination of the illness.

However, Freud noticed that his colleague had also become rather involved with his patient, which led him to ponder whether Breuer's overt concern for Anna represented an unresolved conflict of his own. The reaction to client material by the therapist is the countertransference, and transference is appreciated as a complex interactional dynamic between the therapist and client and as an invaluable therapeutic tool. Working with the transference encourages unconscious thoughts, feelings and associations from the past to be brought into consciousness in the presence of the therapist. Transference occurs, most commonly, when the therapist becomes (represents) a significant other from the client's past, particularly a parental figure.

Although originally countertransference was thought to be a hindrance to effective therapy, it's now regarded as very useful. Because countertransference is noted rather than acted upon (the counsellor is always vigilant regarding their own feelings and reactions), it provides the counsellor with insight into the problems of the client that perhaps would otherwise go unrecognized. The counsellor might think, 'Why do I feel disapproving?' and make the link with what has been said about the client's father, and this would give the opportunity to explore these feelings further. Countertransference feelings are often brought to life in supervision and are frequently a source of discussion in relation to the counsellor's own unresolved emotional difficulties.

## Resistances and defences

A major part of the psychodynamic technique is analysing the resistances that put up a smoke screen to protect the defences. Clients demonstrate resistance in various ways: for example, by being late for sessions; by wanting to finish the therapy in a 'flight to health' (a claim that all their problems are miraculously solved); by missing sessions; and by denial when a counsellor makes accurate observations or interpretations. The resistance betrays a reluctance to discover more, to let down a barrier or open up a protected part of themselves. There are ambivalent feelings: the person wants on the conscious level to have insight into the problems that brought them into counselling in the first place and to deal with life in a more productive self-fulfilling way, but on an unconscious or preconscious level they value and automatically want to hold on to their defences. A skilled, sensitive counsellor respects a client's defence mechanisms and tries to understand the underlying reasons, interpreting them tentatively and gently exploring possibilities in step with the client, who gains self-insight by making subtle shifts in perception.

An analytic tool of free association was introduced by Freud to access the unconscious and interpret defences and resistances. Freud encouraged his patients to talk freely about every thought, feeling, image, memory and association that came into their head, however irrelevant, trivial or disagreeable it seemed. In doing so the patient was likely to let out slips of the tongue (hence the term 'Freudian slip'), making associations that could then be interpreted to bring repressed material into consciousness.

The interpretation of dreams is another technique employed in bringing unconscious material into consciousness. Freud saw dreams as 'wish fulfilment'; but in dreams too there is a certain amount of repression that forms the latent dream content. The latent dream thoughts are transformed into the manifest dream content by self-censoring functions of the individual's mental activity. The psychodynamic counsellor also uses dreams to, as Freud put it, 'unravel what the dream-work has woven'.

## _The therapeutic relationship_

The psychodynamic counsellor adopts a neutral stance based on the 'blank screen' of traditional Freudian psychoanalysis, adopting what's referred to as 'the rule of neutrality', involving a respect for the client's autonomy and an attitude of caring commitment on the part of the counsellor. The 'rule of abstinence' employed by the counsellor is sometimes misunderstood by clients as an attempt by the counsellor to maintain a superior professional distance. The psychodynamic counsellor does not self-disclose, viewing this kind of interaction as detracting from client material. The more a client gets to know the therapist (in the usual sense), the less likely they're able to project and transfer feelings from the past on to them. It's a kind of withholding on the part of the counsellor, but not without reason and therapeutic value; the counsellor holds back rather than engaging in conversation, allowing the client to go on talking and revealing their thoughts and accompanying feelings.

Maintaining boundaries is an important aspect of this approach, involving clear contracting regarding, for instance, frequency and length of sessions and duration of therapy, and creating a confidential and private environment. Assessments and history taking form a baseline of information about the client's early family relationships and experiences. The ending of therapy also has a special significance in this approach – it's likely to stir up past feelings of abandonment and loss that can resurface in last-minute transference feelings. As we've already seen, a central focus of the work is the interpretation of defences and resistances that are brought to the client's attention and confronted with the counsellor. Links are made between past and present and special attention is paid to the client's perceptual world, not only to real experiences but also to how reality is perceived. Increasingly, the psychodynamic counsellor has adopted person-centred values of warmth, acceptance and empathic responding and an interest in presenting themselves as a 'whole' person. The counsellor's own self-development and understanding is a crucial component of the approach. Because personal therapy is encouraged, the psychodynamic counsellor, of course, will have experience of being on the receiving end of therapy as a client, working with transference, exploring childhood material and confronting defences.

## Aim of therapy

The psychodynamic counsellor's view of the 'disturbed' person is someone whose everyday functioning is governed by inner conflicts. The psychoanalytic viewpoint understands everyone to have inner conflicts – the point being that normally they're satisfactorily suppressed and therefore manageable. The person experiencing unmanageable difficulties in their life might know something is wrong but not *what* is wrong, whereas the person who functions in a psychologically satisfied way is untroubled by inner conflict in as much as it's manageable and doesn't dominate their life. A central aim is to help the client to become more self-aware and to bring what's unconscious into consciousness. The counsellor's role is to help the client to gain insight and understanding into aspects of the self that were previously unknown. This is achieved by working with unconscious processes, transference, defences, resistances and dreams, to bring conflicts, impulses and feelings to the surface. Emphasis is placed on self-knowledge and insight rather than on attempting to eliminate problems. As Jacobs points out: 'The psychodynamic approach, which the counsellor also shows in action in her or his work with the client, is also often adopted by the client in self-analysis.'

## C. G. Jung

The work of the analytical psychologist Carl Gustav Jung needs to be mentioned as his contribution to the analytic, psychodynamic and transpersonal approaches has been immense (see also Ruth Snowden's *Jung—The Key Ideas*). Like Freud, Jung was a medical doctor (specializing in psychiatry) who became a pioneering figure in psychoanalysis. Freud, who was Jung's senior by 20 years, was impressed by Jung's pioneering work on schizophrenia. He saw the younger man as a protégé and for a period of six years or so they worked in close association, but in time Jung came to regard Freud's theories on the human sexual drive as limited and restrictive to his own work and they parted ways. Jung's work reflected his diverse interests; from a young age he read extensively, gaining knowledge of philosophy, alchemy, astrology, theology and ancient religions. His main interest was the study of psychotic tendencies in individuals who otherwise functioned normally and he looked for answers in the primitive elements of the psyche. The inspiration that he found in the ancient religions influenced his work – for example, his theories of the individual and the collective unconscious which manifest as archetypes in dreams and visions.

He admired Hinduism for the way it integrates concepts of good and evil in the attributes of gods such as Shiva – the creator and the destroyer – because he believed that it's important for our mental health that we acknowledge the negative, largely unexpressed side of the human condition, which he termed 'the shadow'. For Jung mental stability was a matter of balance, balance between the conscious and unconscious aspects of the personality, including feminine and masculine aspects and intellect and emotion.

## Dreams

Jung considered dreams to be a manifestation of the unconscious mind – a bridge between the conscious and the unconscious elements of the human psyche. He regarded dreams as imbued with meaningful information that guided individuals towards what could fulfil and nourish them. Dreams served as a compensatory or self-regulating form of communication from the unconscious mind that gave expression to neglected or unrealized areas of the individual's true self, or gave warnings when an individual strayed from their 'proper path'. The study of alchemy led Jung to understand dreams as a medium for transforming and purifying psychic energy. He believed that, when information relevant and significant to the whole of humankind is imparted, the result is growth and development for individuals as well as at a collective level.

## Psychological types

Jung began his work on psychological types through observing the personality traits and temperamental differences between Alfred Adler and Freud and the differences between himself and the other two. His first classifications of the extrovert and the introvert types can be best understood as a frame of reference. The individual adopts attitudes towards life that affect their experience. The extrovert character inclines towards the external world of other people and environment, while the introverted character is oriented to the inner world. In his later work Jung added four functions that operated the psyche: thinking, feeling, sensation and intuition. Just as extrovert and introvert are opposites, thinking is opposite to feeling, and sensation is opposite to intuition. In the same way as a person was inclined towards either an extroverted or an introverted expression of personality, the individual tends towards being a predominantly thinking rather than a feeling person or is oriented towards sensation rather than to intuition.

## Individuation

What Jung called 'the process of individuation' is essentially an inner journey embarked on in the second part of life. The first part of life is concerned with being under, then freeing oneself from, parental influence and then establishing oneself as an adult in various roles including useful work, partnering and parenting. Having fulfilled this potential (ostensibly by functioning in the external world), the second part of life is when an individual can achieve a synthesis between their conscious and unconscious self by looking inward. Jung believed the self to be the God within — a 'hypothetical point between conscious and unconscious'. Jung regarded individuation to be a natural psychological process.

## The shadow

So that counsellors can facilitate the client's recognition and acceptance of (what they see as) the more unacceptable parts of themselves, counsellors also need to accept (what Jung called) our 'shadow side'. The shadow is to be found in the unconscious part of ourselves and it's often hidden from us. Our shadow represents all the things that we do not or cannot allow ourselves to do or think. It has been likened to the Mr Hyde part of Dr Jekyll. Jung saw the shadow as the primitive, uncontrolled part of ourselves. It's been called the inferior side of ourselves, but perhaps this encourages us to deny it. It's part of us but it's a side that's regarded as uncivilized and antisocial. Jung also used the term to describe characteristics we originally expressed as children but then learned were unacceptable to our parents or society. An example would be: a girl who shows great ability at something that's regarded as traditionally male territory, such as building or engineering, might (through pressure from parents or society) revert to a more widely stereotypically acceptable female domain, such as playing with dolls and nursing. However, the dormant 'antisocial' part of her will remain within her psyche as a source of ill content in her unfulfilled shadow side.

## Archetypes

Jung looked at history and the mythology of ancient civilizations for clues to unravel the human psyche. While working with patients with schizophrenia he noted that the visions that they had were strikingly similar to those in mythology, yet the details of these were known to only a few scholars. There was no explanation as to how the imagery matched so accurately. Jung was to write that archetypes were 'motifs analogous to or identical with those of mythology', and that they were 'found everywhere and at all times in Greek, Egyptian and ancient Mexican myths and in dreams of modern individuals ignorant of such traditions'. He believed this to be more than coincidental. The concept of synchronicity recognizes that there are acausal connections between people, places and occurrences in the world.

## The collective unconscious

Jung coined the term 'collective unconscious' to describe what he considered the true basis of the human psyche. He said that the collective unconscious was 'not individual but common to all humans as the ancestral heritage of possibilities of representation'. Archetypes, he thought, manifest in dreams and visions to help us with human dilemmas. The collective unconscious is like a pool of human situations and experiences that the human psyche can draw on.

## Anima and animus

Jung used the word *anima*, the Latin for 'soul', to mean the feminine aspect of the male unconscious; likewise, the word *animus*, mind or spirit, is the masculine aspect of the female unconscious. Jung introduced the idea of the sexes having qualities of each other – a man having feminine qualities and vice versa. To be whole, a person needs to accept and integrate both aspects.

# Characteristics of the psychoanalytic/psychodynamic approach

## The psychoanalytic/psychodynamic approach...

* works with unconscious processes – dreams, free association and transference
* focuses on defences as a route to understanding underlying anxieties and hidden feelings
* makes connections between the client's past and present
* insists on a 'rule of neutrality' – an abstinent approach where the therapist doesn't self-disclose and is the expert
* makes interpretations for the client
* relies on knowledge of the client's history
* promotes personal understanding.

# 7

# *the humanistic/ person- centred approach*

The American psychologist Carl Rogers was the founder of person-centred counselling. The core conditions that he identified as imperative to the counsellor–client relationship form the backbone of most counselling models. Rogers encouraged counsellors to be themselves, to live their lives dynamically, enabling them to communicate with their clients congruently.

The humanistic counsellor is warm, empathic and open, and works in partnership with the client to empower them to become what Rogers termed 'a fully functioning individual' and to reconcile inner and outer selves. The person-centred approach is above all an optimistic, loving form of therapy, emerging from the progressive mentality of the 1960s – a period of free expression. Its emphasis on respecting clients contributed greatly to the establishment of clients' rights in therapy and counselling.

## Origins

Abraham Maslow is usually accredited with the title of 'father of humanistic psychology', which reached prominence in the USA in the 1950s and 1960s. Maslow is perhaps best known for his 'hierarchy of needs' model.

The model identifies five basic human needs, here listed in the order of importance:

1 The physiological needs – these are the basic needs for continuing life; for example, water, oxygen, foodstuffs, a need for activity, sleep, bodily elimination, avoidance of pain, sexual expression.

2 Safety and security – these are secondary to the absolute necessities; when the physiological needs are met, then a second layer of needs becomes prominent (e.g. safety, stability, structure, boundaries).

3 Love and belonging – the third layer in Maslow's hierarchy concerns close relationships with others (e.g. bonding, having a place in community). A negative response is a movement towards social anxieties and alienation/loneliness.

4 Self-esteem – Maslow identified two 'esteem needs'. Lower esteem refers to a need for respect from others, for status, attention, appreciation and at times dominance. Higher esteem needs are self-generated (e.g. self-respect, sense of achievement, self-sufficiency, independence).

5 To self-actualize – Maslow equates self-actualization with 'growth motivation' – a continuing desire to 'be all that you can be', which involves a need to fulfil personal potential. However, self-actualization is unlikely to be possible until the lower needs have been met. The self-actualized person is someone who is 'reality centred' – able to differentiate between what's real or genuine and what's 'phoney' or dishonest; 'problem-centred' – essentially problem solving and solution oriented; and resistant to 'enculturation' – unyielding to social pressure.

The humanistic approach to therapy was named the 'third force'. Maslow is also credited with introducing the 'fourth force', transpersonal psychology. Maslow regarded psychology, in the form of psychoanalysis, to be overly concerned with the neurotic and disturbed, and preferred to work with healthy, creative individuals. He also considered the reductionist, mechanistic theory of behaviouralism to be limited in its view of human functioning. What interested him was 'higher human motivation'. Maslow, along with other humanistic psychologists such as Fritz Perls and Eric Berne, was heavily influenced by the philosophy of European existentialists and phenomenologists such as Sartre, Kierkegaard, Husserl and Binswanger. Existentialism rejects the idea of a person as a product of heredity or environment, believing instead that individuals are responsible for their own destiny.

## The person-centred approach

The person-centred approach is the main representation of the humanistic approach presented here because its core conditions model, and many of its ideas, have been widely integrated into other approaches. The views of Carl Rogers and his contemporaries have highly influenced people's attitudes towards therapy. Unlike the cognitive behavioural approaches, the person-centred model is non-directive and focuses on the quality of therapy, especially the therapist's attitude towards the client. Rogers and his associates shifted clinical models in psychology away from the medically oriented model. He developed 'client-centred therapy' in the USA in the 1940s and 1950s, working in educational and pastoral settings, but it was in the liberal 'flower power' climate of the 1960s that it really came to the fore. Experimental encounter groups became popular at this time and well into the 1970s as a method of working in the 'here and now'.

## The Rogerian core conditions model

In a paper entitled 'The Necessary and Sufficient Conditions of Therapeutic Personality Change', Rogers set out a set of six conditions that he regarded as necessary and sufficient to initiate 'constructive personality change':

1 Two persons are in psychological contact.
2 The first, whom we shall term the client, is in a state of incongruence, being vulnerable or anxious.
3 The second person, whom we shall term the therapist, is congruent or integrated in the relationship.
4 The therapist experiences unconditional positive regard for the client.
5 The therapist experiences an empathic understanding of the client's internal frame of reference and endeavours to communicate this experience to the client.
6 The communication to the client of the therapist's empathic understanding and unconditional positive regard is to a minimal degree achieved.

Rogers goes on to conclude: 'No other conditions are necessary. If these six conditions exist, and continue over a period of time, this is sufficient. The process of constructive personality change will follow.'

In Rogerian theory, and to person-centred therapists generally, the relationship between the counsellor and client in the 'here and now' is all important. With this in mind, let's look briefly at how Rogers himself defined what has been narrowed down to the three core values or conditions from his original model; that is, congruence, unconditional positive regard and empathy.

## Congruence

Rogers equated congruence with genuineness – the therapist's ability to be genuine with the client in the relationship. He wrote that the therapist should be 'a congruent, genuine, integrated person'. By 'integrated' he meant 'whole'; that the counsellor or therapist requires self-awareness and is comfortable with their own experiencing, both positive and negative. The therapist doesn't hide behind a professional façade but is 'freely and deeply himself'. To put it in another way, using another Rogerian term, the counsellor is in touch with and able to be their 'authentic self'. This requires the therapist to be open about their feelings in relation to the client and the relationship.

## Unconditional positive regard

This term was used by Rogers to describe a thorough, caring acceptance of the client. He wrote: 'To the extent that the therapist finds himself experiencing a warm acceptance of each aspect of the client's experience as being a part of that client, he is experiencing unconditional positive regard.' Rogers spoke of 'prizing' the person and of accepting the client as a worthwhile human being. To have unconditional positive regard towards another person means there are no conditions of acceptance, which calls for a non-judgemental attitude rather than a selective, evaluating attitude of accepting some aspects of the client while rejecting others. This stance requires the counsellor to be as accepting of the client's negative expression of 'bad' feelings (e.g. fearfulness, hurt, defensiveness, anger) as of 'good' feelings (e.g. competency, confidence, positive social feelings) and to accept inconsistency of behaviour.

## Empathy

'To sense the client's private world as if it were your own, but without ever losing the "as if" quality' is how Rogers described empathic understanding. Empathizing with a person involved, 'sensing' the client's subjective, perceptual world – fears, anger, and confusion – as if they were the counsellor's own, but without 'getting bound up in it'. He wrote of the empathic therapist being able to move around freely in the client's world, helping the client to clarify thoughts, feelings and meanings; and also voicing 'meanings in the client's experience of which the client is scarcely aware'.

Rogers had an optimistic view of humankind; he believed natural human characteristics to be positive, forward-moving, constructive, realistic and trustworthy, and that every organism instinctively moves towards the fulfilment of its inherent potential. Unlike the psychoanalysts who considered the individual to be a mass of antisocial aggressive impulses that needs to be repressed,

Rogers regarded the human as having a deep need for 'affiliation and communication with others'. To become fully socialized, he believed that a person needs first to be fully themselves. Each person is considered to be unique. Person-centred practitioners regard the human personality to be complex and diverse, resisting diagnostic labelling or prescriptive interpretation.

## Self-concept

So, you may ask, what goes wrong? Although the person-centred approach doesn't focus specifically on childhood experiences as a source of unearthing repressed material, as in the psychodynamic approach, it does acknowledge that many aspects of a false self are formed by the individual's need to fit into family and society. Through the process of socialization and what Rogers termed 'conditions of worth' (the self-concept of the child formed by parental and societal values), the potential to become a 'fully functioning' unique person is quashed. In an attempt to satisfy the need for positive regard, the child learns to please others, understanding primarily what aspects of character and self-expression are acceptable to their parents and those around them. Alterations are made and those 'sides' of the self that are unapproved or rejected outright are gradually replaced by behaviour (as expressions of personality) that elicits approval.

## Incongruence

Problems arise when the self – accepted and valued by significant others, first parents, then other social groups, friends or a partner – is incongruent with the 'authentic self'. A state of incongruence has established itself within the individual's self-concept when feelings of inner experiencing are at odds with the self that's presented to the external world. A common example of this is the sensitive boy child who, from a very early age, internalizes parental disapproval of any display of emotion. He experiences parental disapproval and rejection when he cries or shows affection or dependency, and yet he senses that he is met with enthusiastic approval when he is 'being brave', keeping emotions in, being independent and self-contained. He might crave closeness with others all his life but be unable to show emotion or dependence on another person. At the primary stage of his functioning, when he required unconditional love from his parents, he was given acceptance and love only if he met their requirements.

## Locus of evaluation

The self-concept is how we learn to define ourselves to meet the criteria required for us to be loved and valued. A 'fully functioning' person would demonstrate congruence between their inner world of feelings and sensations and outer expression, evident in emotions and behaviour. The congruent person has a strong self-concept, is able to be open, honest with themselves and others, and to live spontaneously. Rogers identified two ways we make judgements or evaluations: from our inner 'locus of evaluation' – the 'centre of responsibility' which lies within us – and through external evaluations – the attitudes or belief systems of others (parents, society, etc.). When a person acts on their own internal evaluations, those that come from feelings and intuition (gut feelings), they are in touch with the 'organismic valuing process', an authentic part of the self, not governed by the values of other people or by institutionalized values. The individual who loses touch with their internal locus of evaluation lives their life by people pleasing, continually focusing on externally defined beliefs and attitudes. A central aim of the person-centred therapist is to help the client reconnect with their inner valuing processes, to understand what they really feel, what changes they would like to make. The person is ideally then freed from introjected values and self-concepts, and begins to appreciate their individuality.

## Becoming a person

The fully functioning or 'actualized' person is in this way in touch with their inner world – the personal self-concept is extended not only to 'this is what I am' but also to 'this is what I can become'. Rogers talked of the individual becoming everything they 'can be', meaning having fulfilment, integration and acceptance of all the parts of their character, being able to find expression in love and work – to reach their full potential. It can be seen as impossible to reach this utopian state of personhood, but it is a striving, an ideal and a continuum. Rogers called it 'the good life' – the world of the fully functioning person whose capacity for interpersonal communication is enhanced through positive self-concept and creative interaction with others. The main aim of 'becoming a person', in the Rogerian sense, is to be in a state of full experiencing; being congruent, able to act on our own feelings, guided by our own organismic valuing processes, and living in the 'here and now'. The concept of 'person in process' is central to the approach.

## *The therapeutic relationship*

While the psychoanalyst endeavours to be a 'blank screen' on to which the patient's transferential material can be projected, humanists regard the willingness of the therapist to engage warmly with the client to be a necessity for therapeutic change. The quality of the interpersonal relationship – supportive, warm, empathic, accepting – provides a safe, validating environment for the client to explore, examine and accept the whole of their self. So that the client feels safe enough to express themselves freely within the therapy, they need to feel equal to and valued by the therapist. Rogers argued that the neutral stance of the psychoanalyst could be interpreted by the client as hostility or rejection, confirming the client's negative self-concept, particularly with regard to their relationships with others.

The person-centred view is that, unless a client perceives the therapist as trustworthy and dependable, the therapeutic engagement will not take place. To be able to convey a trustworthiness the therapist must trust in themselves, in their own ability to experience fully in the 'here and now'; full acceptance of the other person requires the counsellor's acceptance of themselves. Unlike other approaches, the person-centred perspective doesn't rely on complex theories of human personality, nor does the therapist hide behind the professional mask of 'expert'. They engage wholeheartedly in an egalitarian relationship with the client.

# Aim of therapy

Problems, conflicts, confusions and other presenting issues brought to therapy are seen as a manifestation of incongruence in the client's behaviour and experiencing. The authentic self lies buried beneath introjected (parental, other significant figures and institutionalized) 'conditions of worth'. The 'real' or 'authentic' self has kowtowed to outside 'loci of evaluation' to the extent that it has been lost, and the unhappiness and frustrations experienced in living under this mantle are indicative of a need to reclaim the loss. A central aim is to help the client make contact with the organismic centre of their being, to help them re-experience a sense of self-worth and make movement towards changes in their lives. Signs of movement are:

* The client begins to be less concerned with other people's attitudes and judgements and begins to trust in and value their own.
* They increasingly enjoy living in the present and appreciate the process of personal growth and expression rather than being governed by impersonal objectives.
* They demonstrate greater respect for others and self, showing a deep understanding of others and self.
* A valuing of intimacy and close relationships with others.
* A valuing of honesty and 'realness' in self and others.
* Accepting responsibility for their own life.
* A capacity to make considered choices with regard to the direction taken, and to live with a new spontaneity and enjoyment of life.

# 8

# *the behavioural/ cognitive behavioural approach*

Behavioural therapy follows the basic assumption that some psychological problems are acquired through learning experiences and are subsequently maintained by the pattern of events. Its method of treatment focuses on the challenge and reversal of the negative or ineffective learned experiences. Traditionally, behaviourists are less concerned with the abstract (such as feelings) and there has been little emphasis on the therapist–client relationship. Unlike psychoanalysts, behaviourists regard the symptom (for example, a phobia or compulsive behaviour) as the problem, not the underlining causes. The development of cognitive behavioural therapy (CBT), however, has promoted a supportive, more collaborative relationship between the therapist and client as well as a less deterministic view of an individual's behaviour.

In this chapter we will look at the origins of behaviourist thought as a more 'scientific' alternative to the psychoanalytical therapies of Freud and Jung and the development in the late twentieth century of the popular therapy CBT, which added practical insights into human thought patterns and beliefs.

# *Origins*

Cognitive behavioural therapy (widely known as CBT) is commonly placed under the umbrella of the behavioural school of therapy. CBT is considered a branch of behaviour therapy but its origins are also in cognitive therapy. CBT is a product of cognitive theories and techniques and behavioural experimentation. Cognitive therapy originated in the 1960s and two therapists, Aaron Beck and Albert Ellis, are recognized as the main innovators of the cognitive school of therapy and their theories and techniques remain central to cognitive behavioural therapy. Behavioural therapy is a strong influence of CBT and it would be useful to look at a potted history of the behavioural approach to therapy (before we move on to look at CBT) as behavioural and cognitive ideas are integrated in contemporary CBT.

## Behavioural therapy

Behavioural therapy, in its various forms, originated from the scientific discipline of psychology. At the turn of the century and in the early 1900s, psychologists like John B. Watson and Edward L. Thorndike conducted experiments on animals to observe their behaviour. They considered the methods of psychoanalysis and introspection, which prevailed at the time, to be unreliable, based as they were on the subjective, inner thought processes of the patient – an area that was neither measurable nor observable and therefore considered unscientific. Thorndike was influenced by Charles Darwin's theory of evolution and the laws of 'the survival of the fittest' and believed that parallels could be drawn between animal and human behaviour. He went on to systematize a theory of human behaviour, based on the observation of animal behaviour, in laboratory experiments. Watson, accredited with coining the term 'behavioural psychology', also believed that research and a body of empirical evidence would lead to psychology being regarded as a scientific practice.

Watson, who termed himself a behaviourist in 1919, was the forerunner of Burrhus F. Skinner (well known for his development of operant conditioning). The main concern of Watson and his contemporaries was the process of learning; they surmised that the basic principle of learning applied to all organisms, including human beings. They believed that, just as behaviour is learned, it can also be unlearned. Traditional behaviourism understands all human behaviour to be determined by learning through classical and operant conditioning. 'Inappropriate', 'dysfunctional' and 'maladaptive' are all terms used to describe behaviour that can be changed through a process of unlearning.

It wasn't until the end of the Second World War, when psychiatric services were stretched to their limits, that behavioural psychology moved from its scientific research base to practical use as a form of therapy. At this time, B. F. Skinner refined Thorndike's theory of operant conditioning, and it was his version that was widely adopted by behaviourists. Behavioural theory is based on two experimental paradigms: Skinner's operant conditioning and Pavlov's dogs, used to demonstrate classical conditioning.

## Operant and classical conditioning

Thorndike used the term **operant conditioning** to describe behaviour that is largely determined by its consequences. He noted that animals learned responses because they affected their environment. Following a particular behaviour led to a reward of some kind — for example, touching a latch resulted in food becoming available. The learning of a task was strengthened when an action resulted in reward. Thorndike termed this the 'law of effect' and understood it in terms of trial and error on the part of animals rather than an innate intelligence, linking his observations with Darwin's theory of evolutionary selection; that is, species that adapt to their surroundings adapt their behaviour and therefore stand a greater chance of survival.

Skinner built on the work of Thorndike and it was his method of studying operant conditioning that was eventually widely adopted. Skinner's theory was based on the idea of reinforcements playing a motivational role in the learning of new tasks. Positive reinforcement describes the strengthening of a response by the incentive of a stimulus as reward. Negative reinforcement describes the strengthening of a response by removing an unpleasant stimulus (e.g. a loud noise). Reinforcements can be food, stroking, praise or encouragement. Gradually the animal would recognize that certain behaviour ended in favourable results, which led to a mastering of the task. In contrast, an operantly conditioned response is based on the premise that if something isn't reinforced it will gradually die out – this is referred to as 'extinction' in behavioural terminology.

A definition of **classical conditioning** is: 'One particular event follows another.' In the early 1900s a Russian psychologist called Ivan Pavlov held experiments to observe the associative learning of animals. A famous experiment involving dogs, a meat dispenser and a light demonstrated different responses to stimuli. Unconditional responses were replaced by conditional responses to stimulus through a process of association. Over a period of time a neutral stimulus (e.g. the light) is associated with a reflexive stimulus (food) – even when food is no longer dispensed – resulting in a conditional response (e.g. salivation) to the neutral stimulus alone.

## _Problems tackled by behavioural therapy_

Widely used in the treatment of anxiety, phobic and obsessive compulsive disorders and sexual dysfunctions, behavioural therapy also lends itself to social learning programmes in child development and to helping to extend social and communication skills in adults who exhibit inappropriate, dysfunctional behaviour.

### Treatment plan

Behavioural treatment incorporates a variety of techniques that aim to solve problems by bringing measurable and observable change to the client's behaviour, altering behaviour patterns in specific currently dysfunctional areas. The treatment is modified to suit each individual's needs. In the case of panic attacks or phobias, the exposure principle is followed where the client is gradually exposed to the disturbing object or situation (gradual emersion) in a process called systematic desensitization. This technique has been widely used to treat phobic and obsessional compulsive disorders and is used in CBT. There are two types of exposure:

1 Vivo exposure – when the actual feared object or situation is confronted.

2 Imaginal or fantasy exposure – this entails imaging the act of dealing with the problem while in a state of relaxation. The behaviourist Joseph Wolpe pioneered the technique of pairing relaxation with the troubling conditioned stimuli.

The client is given 'homework' in the form of tasks between sessions. Goals are discussed and negotiated. The client is also often asked to keep a diary to note progress and setbacks.

Because phobias and other forms of anxiety disorder are accompanied by physiological ('fight or flight') responses such as sweating, heart palpitations and dizziness, Wolpe suggested the use of relaxation in the form of progressive muscle relaxation to help the client gain control over the anxiety-producing condition. First the client would be trained during therapy sessions, by the therapist, in the relaxation techniques; then, when these became familiar to the client, they could be self-applied in stressful anxiety-producing situations. Wolpe recommended deep relaxation as an anxiety-inhibiting response because he believed that we can't experience deep relaxation and fear concurrently. The same practices are used in adapted forms today.

## Cognitive behavioural therapy (CBT)

Cognitive science emerged partly in response to behaviourism's deterministic view of human behaviour, which some therapists criticized as reducing the human being and human consciousness to the level of the machine. The central focus of cognitive approaches is the individual's thought patterns and beliefs, and how these link with self-defeating behaviour. Clients are helped to change the way they think; irrational, self-destructive thoughts are replaced by more realistic and helpful thoughts.

The underlying principals of the cognitive behavioural theory (CBT) approach include:

* A collaborative therapeutic relationship – as an active form of therapy, there is emphasis on therapist and client co-operation.
* Structure and goal orientation – CBT is a highly structured and problem-focused way of working, and goals and tasks are identified and agreed upon by clients and counsellor.
* Development of self-help – CBT relies on client motivation and willingness to take part in homework tasks. The client is coached in the techniques and skills of the approach.
* Cognitive techniques and behavioural experiments – elements of both approaches inform CBT concepts and practical application.
* Empiricism – based on experience, experiment and observation, the approach is well tested through extensive experiments, research and studies. Clients test for themselves the effectiveness of change, noting how their thinking affects their emotions and behaviour.

## Aaron Beck

Aaron Beck, one of the founders of cognitive therapy, began his professional life as a psychoanalytic psychotherapist. In his work he came to the conclusion that an individual's cognitions (i.e. mental messages) affect both feeling and behaviour. He noted the irrationality behind self-critical cognitions, which he called 'automatic thoughts'. These are also sometimes termed negative automatic thoughts (NATs).

The psychoanalytic understanding of emotional disturbance, or behavioural dysfunctioning, is that it is rooted in unresolved trauma from childhood. In contrast, the cognitive approach considers problems to arise not directly from the events themselves but from how the individual interprets and creates meaning for them. Another difference between the two approaches is that while psychoanalysis considers thought to be dictated by emotional needs, cognitive behaviourists believe it is cognitive processes that govern the emotions. Cognitive behavioural counsellors use a model of cognitive processing called the cognitive distortion model devised by Beck. In this model Beck proposed that, when a person perceives a situation to be threatening, it results in a reduction in reasoning and functioning of normal cognitive processes.

Cognitive (thinking) distortions include:

* **All or nothing thinking** – thinking in absolutes
* **Crystal ball gazing** – negatively predicting the future
* **Emotional reasoning** – assuming negative emotions as reality
* **Discounting the positive** – dismissing positive experiences
* **Jumping to conclusions** – making a negative assumption with no evidence to support it
* **Labelling** – naming a behaviour as a personality trait
* **Magnification or catastrophizing** – blowing things out of proportion, exaggerating things
* **'Should' and 'must' statements** – tyrannical demands we make of ourselves

Do any of the above seem familiar? Most of us will identify with many of these kinds of distorted ways of thinking.

## Albert Ellis

Albert Ellis, who along with Aaron Beck is regarded as a founder of cognitive therapy, went on to establish rational emotive behaviour therapy (REBT). Ellis, like Beck, originally trained as a psychoanalyst. REBT (also referred to as RET) adopts a robust directive therapeutic style that challenges and confronts the 'irrational beliefs' of clients. 'Crooked thinking' governed by 'shoulds' and 'musts' was, in the opinion of Ellis, the cause of emotional problems and maladaptive behaviour. Internalized irrational beliefs lead to 'catastrophizing', anxiety and depression; 'catastrophizing' means to view things in an absolutistic, exaggerated or overstated manner – an 'it's the end of the world' scenario. In REBT and in CBT the client is helped to change their irrational beliefs to more rational statements, thereby enabling them to deal with problems constructively.

Ellis's ABC theory is central to CBT:

**A** – represents the activating event – a person's action, attitude or an actual physical event.

**B** – represents the belief the person has about the event.

**C** – represents the consequence of the event, in terms of the individual's emotions and behaviour in relation to their experiencing of the event.

The CBT counsellor or therapist teaches the client, through the ABC formula, how to engage in metacognitive processing of their thoughts in relation to events. Cognitive reactions to events can be monitored, reflected on and understood, giving the client more choice of perspective.

In Ellis's theory it isn't A, the activating event, that causes C, the consequence, but rather it is B, the client's beliefs, that colour the relationship between the event and the consequence (i.e. the resultant feelings and conduct). For example, one person might believe that a missed opportunity means that all opportunities are now closed to them and, feeling depressed, give up trying to achieve their goal; while another person might think the missed opportunity is one of many that will come their way and feels OK about the situation, continuing to work towards their goal.

Cognitive theories were added to the behavioural approach to therapy because therapists realized that cognitions (e.g. thoughts, beliefs, perceptions) played a major part in individual experiencing. Behavioural and cognitive practices have merged as the two are acknowledged to complement each other. The combined theories have produced a therapeutic approach for the treatment, in particular, of depressive and anxiety states. As a scientific therapeutic approach that relies on observation and monitoring (of behaviour and cognitions), the model has been widely endorsed and adopted by the medical professions. A central aim of cognitive behavioural therapy is to replace negative beliefs and automatic thoughts with realistic self-accepting beliefs that are more self-affirming. With the counsellor's help, the client learns to monitor and gain control of how they think and behave.

## The therapeutic relationship

A criticism of behaviourism has been that, in an approach built on empirical investigation (knowledge based on experimental research), the therapist has taken a clinically detached and highly directive role. The client could easily be made to feel powerless or worthless. Although traditionally the client–therapist relationship has not been considered central to these modes of therapy, more recently in cognitive behavioural therapy it has been recognized that the relationship is important, for several reasons:

* The co-operation of the client is necessary because the approach is task and target oriented requiring negotiation.
* In a supporting role, the therapist needs to demonstrate that they are trustworthy, warm and accepting, as well as directive, as the client's motivation could depend on encouragement and praise.
* Therapist-aided tasks (when the therapist accompanies the client on anxiety-inducing tasks) necessitate sensitive communication. Client and therapist work closely together and trust is essential.
* The therapist teaches or coaches the client in the use of skills and techniques, helping them gain insight into how they function and guides them towards 'self-therapy'.

Sometimes a member of the family acts as a co-therapist whose role it is to support and encourage. The co-therapist will be guided by the therapist and informed as to progress and difficulties.

The cognitive behavioural counsellor uses various techniques to assess cognitions, including asking the client to apply methods of monitoring self-statements by:

* thinking out loud while doing a task
* working with a tape recorder to record spontaneous talk
* completing worksheets to record, for example, details of the activating events, belief and behavioural consequences/outcome.

Once the client becomes aware of their beliefs and automatic thoughts they can begin, with the guidance and encouragement of the counsellor, to experiment with alternative (more balanced) beliefs or self-statements in relation to particular events.

## Aim of therapy

The focus of work is to bring to the client's awareness cognitions that can be either appropriate or inappropriate, functional or dysfunctional, constructive or destructive, rational or irrational, adaptive or maladaptive. In simple terminology, cognitions can either work for us or against us, and the cognitive behaviourist helps the client make changes to lessen, if not totally eradicate, negative self-messages and their effects.

## Characteristics of the behavioural/ cognitive approach

### The behavioural/cognitive approach...

* is a highly structured approach that's effective in addressing problems
* is collaborative
* calls upon the therapist to act as an educator and coach
* encourages self-awareness and self-responsibility
* makes links between thoughts, moods and actions
* provides practical coping strategies and skills
* can be combined with other approaches.

For a more in-depth exploration of CBT, see *Cognitive Behavioural Therapy* in the *Teach Yourself* series.